D0498370

THE DECLINE OF THE
SECULAR UNIVERSITY

19.80

THE DECLINE OF THE SECULAR UNIVERSITY

C. John Sommerville

UNIVERSITY PRESS
2006

OXFORD
UNIVERSITY PRESS

Oxford University Press, Inc., publishes works that further
Oxford University's objective of excellence
in research, scholarship, and education.

Oxford   New York
Auckland   Cape Town   Dar es Salaam   Hong Kong   Karachi
Kuala Lumpur   Madrid   Melbourne   Mexico City   Nairobi
New Delhi   Shanghai   Taipei   Toronto

With offices in
Argentina   Austria   Brazil   Chile   Czech Republic   France   Greece
Guatemala   Hungary   Italy   Japan   Poland   Portugal   Singapore
South Korea   Switzerland   Thailand   Turkey   Ukraine   Vietnam

Published by Oxford University Press, Inc.
198 Madison Avenue, New York, New York 10016

www.oup.com

Oxford is a registered trademark of Oxford University Press

Library of Congress Cataloging-in-Publication Data
Sommerville, C. John (Charles John), 1938–
The decline of the secular university / C. John Sommerville.
p. cm.
Includes bibliographical references and index.
ISBN-13 978-0-19-530695-8
ISBN 0-19-530695-3
1. Universities and colleges—United States—Religion.
2. Church and college—United States.   I. Title.
LC383.S66 2006
378.73—dc22   2005032466

3 5 7 9 8 6 4 2

Printed in the United States of America
on acid-free paper

To
DONALD AND CECILIA CATON
and
JAY AND LAURA LYNCH

PREFACE

As sometimes happens, since I first sent this manuscript to the press, things have happened to underscore some of the points it makes.

First, the *Chronicle of Higher Education* reported that when Jacques Derrida died, Stanley Fish, the dean of American "postmodernists," was asked what he thought would be the Next Big Thing in the academy after race, class, and gender. He had no hesitation in saying "religion," declaring that just studying *about* religion, the only permitted approach till now, is being effectively challenged by those who are more open-minded on the subject. He thought that more and more intellectuals are questioning the distinctions that have constrained the officially secular university in assessing what counts as knowledge.[1]

A couple of months later came the news that Professor Antony Flew, Britain's most prominent philosophical atheist, at age eighty-one had adjusted his lifelong (un)belief to something more like Deism. He was now quoting Einstein approvingly: "Certainly it is a conviction, akin to a religious feeling, of the rationality or intelligibility of the world [that] lies behind all scientific work of a higher order. . . . This firm belief, a belief bound up with deep feeling, in a superior mind that reveals itself in the world of experience, represents my conception of God." Flew had been impressed by a consideration of the so-called Anthropic Coincidences of current physics, which "prove" nothing but can count as "confirming evidence."[2] The introduction to a new edition of his *God and Philosophy* acknowledged he was still having to consider these matters.[3]

1. "One University, Under God?" *Chronicle of Higher Education* 51 (7 January 2005), C1.
2. Interview on BBC Radio 3, 22 March 2005.
3. Antony Flew, *God and Philosophy* (Amherst, NY: Prometheus, 2005), 9–17.

Finally, novelist Tom Wolfe's portrayal of some of the repellent aspects of university life in *I Am Charlotte Simmons* was being discussed where I worked. One reviewer, who had worked at the university that provided Wolfe's setting, noted that the "vision of higher education as a place where the young are initiated into the wisdom of the past has turned into a place where the old abandon the young to their own meager resources because the old have nothing of value to say to them."[4]

In this book we will be searching for some keys to the disappointing condition of our modern universities, in comparison to the hopes with which they began just over a century ago.

The germ of some of my arguments appeared in papers I gave at a conference titled "The Future of Christianity in the West," at the University of Otago, New Zealand, in 2002, and at two conferences at Baylor University, "Moral Formation in American Higher Education," in 2003, and "Christianity and the Soul of the University," in 2004. Thanks go to Al Zambone for an invitation to participate. Bits of the chapters have been published in "Post-Secularism Marginalizes the University: A Rejoinder to Hollinger," *Church History* 71 (2002): 848–857, and "Secularism at Bay," *First Things* 134 (June/July 2003): 11–13.

I owe much to Cynthia Read of Oxford University Press and to the invaluable suggestions of two anonymous readers. Finally, I have been stimulated by involvement with Dr. Richard Horner, Director of the Christian Study Center of Gainesville (Florida), and others there and at the University of Florida, who offered criticisms of views I first tried out on them.

---

4. William H. Willimon, in *Christian Century* (19 April 2005), 21.

CONTENTS

THE DECLINE OF THE
SECULAR UNIVERSITY

1

THE MARGINALIZATION OF
OUR UNIVERSITIES

I am asking you to consider a very odd notion: the irrelevance of the secular university in America. We are used to thinking that universities are becoming ever bigger and more important. What possible sense is there in suggesting that the reverse is true?

Consider: if universities are offering political leadership, why has there been the drift to the political right in this country? It is a well-documented fact that university faculties currently lean hard the other way. If universities are exercising cultural leadership, why do they seem more attentive to pop culture than to the high culture they were nurtured in? If universities are offering scientific leadership, why do they mainly hire their labs out to government and business, with the goal being patents? If they are offering social leadership, why don't professors dominate the talk shows that try to embody our "public opinion"? Is it true, as we often hear, that universities have become trade schools, offering the credentials that students prefer to a rounded education? Why are they only maintaining booths in the intellectual marketplace rather than providing leadership of any kind?

Universities come close to forming worlds unto themselves, but they are aware that there is a society out there that goes its own way. Academic elites are exasperated that our elections and our wars seem to involve religions they thought were discredited. They may be disgusted that science fantasy excites their students more than science and that our media now seem more interested in the private sphere than in the public sphere of political decision. Populist bloggers have a following to match that of our accredited elites. Academics have been praising diversity and empowerment for some time now, but they can't have meant *this*. How did things get out of hand?

⌒

In 2000 the scholarly journal *Church History* inaugurated a new feature, which was to let prominent historians submit "thought pieces" that told what they hoped would be the direction of future academic scholarship. The first person chosen was Professor David Hollinger, an intellectual historian at Berkeley. The journal's editors chose him because he is not in sympathy with religious history, and they thought this might prove challenging to their readers. He chose to talk about the university's secularization, or indeed its secularism.

What Hollinger said is that religious historians ought to study secularization more. It's a topic they've been avoiding. Most especially, they should take up the question of why American universities are thoroughly secular, but American society is not. Why is the country out of phase with its intellectuals? It isn't that way in Europe. As he put it, why does secularism win all the arguments, but religion still win the votes? The journal allowed me to respond to Hollinger's piece, which began the following reflections.

My thesis in what follows is, first, that the secular university is increasingly marginal to American society and, second, that this is a *result* of its secularism. In effect, I mean that questions that might be central to the university's mission are too religious for it to deal with. For example:

1 | What is the status of the concept of the human today; have we become unable to justify a distinction between humans and all other life-forms? Does the university's unofficial naturalism really take everything into account, or does it leave out too much? Don't we end up admitting arguments that evoke religious concepts?

2 | Doesn't professional education, which attracts the vast majority of our students, always relate to a view of the human? Don't all professional programs serve some idea of human optimality, involving ethical imperatives that the university shies away from because they raise the specter of religion?

3 | How should we judge between religions, in a day when those differences are clearly becoming more upsetting to the world? Why do universities seem determined to ignore the differences and insinuate a moral equivalency?

4 | Why are we afraid of *requiring* the study of what used to be called "Western Civilization"? Should multiculturalism trump an understanding of the forces, including religious forces, that have shaped us, so that we don't understand ourselves?

5 | Is there really a philosophical justification for the fact/value dichotomy, which was the keystone of secularism throughout the last century?

6 | How does the university justify the moralizing that still dominates the humanities subjects, having given up acknowledged moral judgment?

7 | Isn't it time to begin studying *about* secularism, instead of just indoctrinating students in it, as we now do? Can we now see that it is a stage *within* history rather than the end of history?

And perhaps most disturbing of all:

8 | Why is intellectual fashion replacing reasoned argument in the university itself?

These are some of the subjects I address in this book. They are not trivial. Considering them may indicate why we no longer look to universities for leadership. My suggestions will have to do with widening the university's discourse, even if this involves terms that we recognize as religious.

I do not imagine that we could restore the university to the position its founders imagined for it in 1900. Indeed, I believe that vision was flawed. But perhaps a healing process could begin if the present ideological commitment to secularism was relaxed. Greater actual diversity, where philosopher Alasdair MacIntyre's different "traditions of inquiry" were in actual dialogue, would be more impressive and interesting than the sterile, narrow, and disappointed institutions we have today. So this will not be an exercise in nostalgia for a mythic time when we did all this better. The problems were different in earlier times, our knowledge was different, the understandings of religion may have been different. We should be thinking what the possibilities are for us today, and how things could develop differently.

In doing so, we need not concentrate on what a few elite universities might be doing. After all, my university alone is nearly as large as the Ivy League. The great majority of students attend institutions of middle rank. Their instructors may be trying to imagine what academic leaders are doing and attempting to get in step, but they and their students live in another world. We had a poignant reminder of this in a recent book by philosophy professor Martha Nussbaum of the University of Chicago, formerly of Brown and Harvard. Her *Cultivating Humanity: A Classical Defense of Reform in Liberal Education* is full of thoughtful advice, but one can't help wondering how many students these days could even read it.[1] I notice, for instance, that the markings in my university library's copy cease after the introduction. Professor Nussbaum is performing in front of a mirror. Like many in the upper reaches of our profession, she may fail to see that her audience has vanished.

Professor David Kirp of Berkeley is another educational leader who imagines that universities are still the focus of a respectful public. In a book that worries over the implications of the "marketplace" model of higher education, he speaks of "the Cornel West soap opera [that] made the front pages in newspapers from Boston to LA," referring to the competition to hire a certain black philosopher.[2] That seems dubious. What most papers care about is who tops *US News*'s highly questionable annual rankings, which might as well appear in the sports section. Kirp also imagines that Internet education will be monopolized by "academic superstars," as if the public would know a famous professor from an actor playing one.

So why are universities failing to connect with our deepest interests and our most pressing concerns? In my article, mentioned above, I associated the university's decline with what I called America's "postsecular" condition. Not secular, but postsecular, by which I mean a situation in which cultural fashion has replaced intellectual argument.

1. Martha C. Nussbaum, *Cultivating Humanity: A Classical Defense of Reform in Liberal Education* (Cambridge, MA: Harvard University Press, 1997).
2. David L. Kirp, *Shakespeare, Einstein, and the Bottom Line* (Cambridge, MA: Harvard University Press, 2003), 67, 79.

Secular rationalism itself cannot find traction on the slippery ground of a postsecular culture.

Things looked altogether different a century ago, when the secular university made its appearance in America. In 1910 the prominent historian Frederick Jackson Turner of the University of Wisconsin looked forward to a time when "by training in science, in politics, economics, and history the universities may supply . . . administrators, legislators, judges and experts or commissioners who shall disinterestedly and intelligently mediate between contending interests." He saw hope "in the increasing proportion of university men in legislatures."[3] Woodrow Wilson, president of Princeton, likewise wrote,

> It is the business of a University to train men in . . . the right thought of the world, the thought which it has tested and established, the principles which have stood through the seasons and become at length part of the immemorial wisdom of the race. . . . I believe that the catholic study of the world's literature as a record of spirit is the right preparation for leadership in the world's affairs.[4]

Chancellor Francis H. Snow of the University of Kansas, an entomologist, voiced a commonplace in saying that the university should train body and spirit as well as mind and could do this by fostering an atmosphere conducive to spiritual development.[5] As universities shifted from earlier religious foundations, it seemed that nothing important would be lost.

These voices seem to come from an ancient past. When university presidents must give speeches today, they muse over the threat from extracollegiate technical training and the diminishing useful life of the information their universities offer. The American university is now bigger than ever, better funded, producing more of whatever it pro-

---

3. Quoted in Richard Hofstadter, *Anti-Intellectualism in American Life* (New York: Alfred A. Knopf, 1963), 200.
4. Quoted in George M. Marsden, *The Soul of the American University: From Protestant Establishment to Established Nonbelief* (New York: Oxford University Press, 1994), 226.
5. Clifford S. Griffin, *The University of Kansas: A History* (Lawrence: University Press of Kansas, 1974), 165. Julie A. Reuben says that this was the common aspiration until about 1900; see Reuben, *The Making of the Modern University: Intellectual Transformation and the Marginalization of Morality* (Chicago: University of Chicago Press, 1996), 73.

duces. Young people think they need a degree of some sort in order to participate in society fully. Universities are indeed important for training for our very technical society, although now other institutions are also being developed for this purpose. But universities are not really where we look for answers to our life questions. That is the sense in which they seem marginal.

The way I put it to my students is to ask where in the university they would go to learn how to *spend* their money. We have lots of programs that tell you how to make money and be useful to the economy. But where would you go to learn how to spend your money intelligently? That is, where does one learn what is *valuable in and of itself*? What is the point of money? It is not self-evident, although we increasingly treat it as such.

A century ago, when American universities were taking over from the earlier colleges, they talked about their "civilizing mission." Universities would bring everything together, the sciences and social sciences, the arts and humanities, and the professions. Wisdom and practicality would learn to relate to each other and to the goals of an increasingly complex society. Thus the purposes of money would become clear.

At that time, just before 1900, university reformers seem to have thought that the liberal arts and especially the humanities would replace the more overtly religious core of the earlier colleges, which actually included chapel along with learning. Professors would replace clergy as the official authorities on life's questions. This view had a certain amount of success. Already in 1912 a university president, Woodrow Wilson, was elected president of the United States. As late as the 1950s *Life* magazine carried stories on major intellectuals. I doubt if *People* magazine ever has, and after a century of secularization intellectuals are becoming less visible.

The liberal arts core of that model university has been hollowed out, in two ways. First a dwindling percentage of students graduate in them. The great majority of students are now in professional programs, learning how to make money and be useful. Second, the liberal arts themselves have changed. They've turned into technical specialties. They're often addressing questions nobody is asking, and giving answers nobody can understand.

I hesitate to give local examples, but a couple of years ago the English department at my university held a graduate student symposium called "Rethinking Deconstructions." Among the announced subjects was "How are deconstructions exemplified in your particular projects?" and "How might your current work be recognized in terms of deconstructions?" This would only interest other academics. Why not rather ask, "Would you have trouble explaining your current project to the seatmate on your next flight?" That seatmate is a taxpayer, paying your salary. More important, she has questions about what is important or valuable in life. What will she conclude about academics if it all comes out in obscure jargon? Students, likewise, may be disappointed in the humanities when the point is not the appreciation of culture, but only criticism of culture.

How did we get into this situation, in which universities fail to connect with people's most urgent questions? We will meet many reasons in the chapters to follow. But first let us grant the simple effects of size and specialization. Departments keep subdividing as we learn more. The scale of universities is so vast that they become worlds unto themselves—academic ghettos. We talk only to others within our specialty, and may have trouble doing even that. Faculty members who take their turn on grant committees often shake their heads over the research proposals they must read from alien departments.

We can't just ignore the explosion of knowledge and information that we have to deal with these days. Increasingly, administrators worry that the training we give at the university becomes obsolete so rapidly. The degrees they award mean less as the useful life of "information" shrinks. But why talk only about information? One no longer hears administrators giving talks on "wisdom," an old-fashioned word meaning seeing things in their widest context, including our ultimate concerns. Perhaps we overdid this in the past and don't want to be thought preachy now. But the public still has a sense that universities should be wiser than the rest of us. If academics faced with value decisions say, "We can't decide these matters for you," people must look elsewhere.

But there is something besides size and specialization that is undermining the universities. They have also lost touch with important questions by their secularization. Important questions seem to involve "ultimate" values and standards of reference. One might object that it was secularization that allowed universities to develop without interference from dogmatic authorities. We will propose the view that they overdid it. For as theologian Hans Küng has put it, "There is a growing awareness that the serious problems of human beings, of society, of science and technology, and of ambivalent progress and growth raise questions that relate as never before to reality as a whole."[6]

To have serious arguments you need reference points. It is amazing the extent to which money now serves as our ultimate reference point. We treat it as a self-evident good instead of as a means to some real, actual good. Even universities are often measured in terms of money. If one asks, "What is money a means toward?" the answer is likely to be, "That's up to you. It's not the university's place to tell you." This is what politicians are saying by making tax reduction their top priority: "Nobody knows better than you how to spend your money." And while we're on the subject we can note that as states are restructuring their universities, they may look not to faculty but to leaders from business and politics. Former politicians are being appointed as university presidents. So things have changed since Woodrow Wilson's time. It seems that Kennedy was the last president who looked largely to university faculties to staff his administration.

Many have drawn attention to the secularization of the university. Some have treated this secularization as largely a matter of the specialization that destroyed the sense of the unity of knowledge. Religion could not continue to preside over all fields in the old way.[7] Others have thought it was due to a naive acceptance of naturalism. The problems of such a view were not immediately obvious.[8] Some have pointed out that religious leaders themselves were complicit in abandoning religious elements that seemed an embarrassment. They felt that this was a way to maintain some vestige of their cultural leadership.[9] Still others see

---

6. David Ray Griffin and Joseph C. Hough Jr., eds., *Theology and the University* (Albany: State University of New York Press, 1991), 63.
7. John K. Roberts and James Turner, *The Sacred and the Secular University* (Princeton: Princeton University Press, 2000).
8. Edward A. Purcell Jr., *The Crisis of Democratic Theory: Scientific Naturalism and the Problem of Value* (Lexington: University Press of Kentucky, 1973).
9. Marsden, *Soul of the American University*; James Turner, *The Liberal Education of Charles Eliot Norton* (Baltimore: Johns Hopkins University Press, 1999).

the secularization as a more intentional rejection of religion; they raise the issue of fairness to our population, for religious elements do not see why their views find no recognition in tax-supported institutions.[10] Doubtless there is merit in all of these approaches, but my focus will be on the intellectual loss to the university that this secularization represented. That is, I will be more interested in the university's loss than in any loss that religion has sustained.

There are several terms that we need to be clear about. Technically, secularization is, in the first instance, only the separation of religion from various aspects of life and of thought. It is compatible with high levels of religious belief and practice, so long as they stay to themselves and out of public life. *Secularism* is something different, an ideology that seeks to complete and enforce secularization. So secularization, by itself, may mean a purification of religion, separating its essence from things we think are superstition. Some aspects of secularization have even been encouraged by religions, as Protestantism encouraged the simplification of Christianity in the Reformation.[11] But the ideology of secularism is not satisfied with that; it aims to eliminate religion altogether. The important feature of secularism for my argument is that it is characterized by determinedly rational argument and led by elites. What I am calling postsecularism is the triumph of fashion over this rational argument and the triumph of a kind of cultural democracy over elites. And that, I submit, is the situation now experienced by the university in America.

This country was the first Western nation to have an officially secular basis. In 1800 our Constitution was looked at askance by Europeans, who still thought agreement on ultimate questions, sealed by the establishment of a state church, was a practical requirement of societies. And we have always marginalized religion for the sake of civic peace, given a very diverse society. This does not mean that it is not honored in private life, of course.

---

10. Reuben, *Making of the Modern University*; Christian Smith, ed., *The Secular Revolution* (Berkeley: University of California Press, 2003).
11. C. John Sommerville, *The Secularization of Early Modern England: From Religious Culture to Religious Faith* (New York: Oxford University Press, 1992).

But that benign secularization has left us without "absolute," or at least official, reference points. It has become almost a mantra of the secular university that there are no absolutes. Relativism, the view that ideas and values are relative to larger social and cultural patterns, has become a fundamental assumption. The so-called postmodernists have recently popularized the understanding that there are no self-validating rational principles at the basis of all thinking and that there was something artificial and arbitrary about the old academic rationalism. So it is commonly accepted that logic doesn't take us down to bedrock, but only down to some useful assumptions.

Science seems to be an exception. One might think that science's contribution to secularization was to offer a different set of reference points and to thereby replace religion at the center of our culture. Science surely follows logical principles. And yet we persist in saying that there no absolute truths. We have come to know something of the limits of science. We sense that science and rationality aren't going to give us absolute answers or ultimate truths, or tell us how to spend our money. Science works on a limited range of questions, as we are beginning to understand.

There is something else wrong with science these days: It's too complex. The public can't follow it. We may think we can, when news reports digest it for us. But in fact, science has developed beyond our ability to visualize its realities or read its mathematical formulations. In reaction to this, many feel free to criticize it. And so we enter the postmodern, postsecular world that universities must now deal with.

Scientists are understandably upset about this populist independence. Some have counterattacked in the books entitled *The Higher Superstition* and *The Flight from Science and Reason*. Their point was, you can't just treat science as a servant and go elsewhere for your ideology or beliefs. We may not have all the answers yet, but we will. This was the point of Edward O. Wilson's popular books, like *Consilience*. All knowledge is of a piece, and so all of it is science. We're not finished yet, but what's your alternative?

Wilson's audience seems to want to have it both ways. American society appreciates science and gladly accepts its fruits. But it hasn't turned against religion enough to satisfy Wilson. We are a populist society, and elitist enterprises have a hard time in our cultural democracy. Our students tend to avoid science, and the universities have given up fighting them over this. Mine requires a bare three courses in the hard sciences. Graduate programs in many sciences would be devastated if we couldn't import international students.

What's more, science instruction is becoming ever less philosophical, ever more technical, so that it no longer seems to suggest answers to the big questions. Students might assume a generally naturalistic philosophy, but they would quickly get out of their depth in trying to pursue it to any conclusions.

Thus we appear to have reached a defining moment in our history. Science has been so successful that it can be taken for granted. Our society and our universities are apparently moving from a culture dominated by the search for knowledge to one more concerned with applying the knowledge we have. This has implications for religion and secularism. When the focus of the university was on the discovery of physical reality, the burden of proof was on religious thinkers to show how they were relevant. Now that our universities are devoted to professional education, our questions are about human needs and aspirations. From medicine and law and business to education, art, engineering, pharmacy, agriculture, journalism, and the rest, questions of optimal conditions for humans are at the center of attention. And the burden of proof should shift to scientists to show how all human activity, values, dreams, interests, culture can be explained in terms of, for instance, molecular biology or quantum physics. This is clearly preposterous. Religion has always provided us the language appropriate to these concerns, at least at their ultimate limits. In short, science was never cut out to be the queen of all thought; rather, it is meant to be a servant. That is not an insult or a demotion, just a sign that we must now move on.

To repeat, the secularist stage in history was dominated by epistemology and positivism, when the university's project was knowledge of "the world." Now we are moving into a hermeneutic and personalist stage in which the task is to explore human meanings, where religion may again be relevant. Something like this has happened before, at the end of the medieval period. It was then that the science and the nominalist philosophy of the medieval universities fell into skepticism, discovering the lack of self-validating rational principles at the basis of all knowledge. It was not long before Europe was saved by a new humanism, which revived an interest in rhetoric and in the ethical aspects of religion. This Renaissance was not initially an enemy of the religious reformations of the time. There was nothing essentially irreligious about the early humanists, though they and the religious reformers eventually fell out due to the circumstances of the time.

At the moment Americans seem happy to use science but feel free to go elsewhere with their life questions. Hollinger suggests that things are different in Europe. Of course, far fewer people there have gone to university. They may be more respectful toward their elites and to rationalism, not having seen them up close. Americans have acquired a distinctly casual attitude toward their universities, as seen in the fact that a third of our undergraduates work full time.[12]

Just as elitism and populism have opposite relations to secularism, so they differ on religion. Sociologists have shown that the elitism associated with established churches tends to drag religion down, which is what has happened in Europe. By contrast, the populism of voluntary churches is their strength, and that's what we've got in America. So European elites seem to be helping secularism and hurting religion, while American populism seems to be hurting secularism and helping religion.

There are, of course, doubts about polls that show how religious Americans claim to be. For religion is the fashion here, as it may be the fashion in Europe to admit less religion than one feels. However, it may be that the official secularism of our universities has played a part in making Americans religiously inarticulate. We may not be able to say anything very intelligent about our religious feelings or ideas. Neither can we say anything very intelligent about our philosophical views. Universities are not giving us much practice at formulating worldviews, in its haste to fit us for our jobs.

Students' minds contain fragments of various viewpoints. Depending on the discussion, they might appeal to materialist assumptions (in

---

12. Andrew Delbanco, "Colleges: An Endangered Species," *New York Review of Books* 52 (10 March 2005).

explaining their behavior), humanistic assumptions (in their political complaints), utilitarian ones (in describing their ambitions), romantic ones (about their music), scientistic ones (in countering religion), religious ones (in refuting other religious positions). All of these may seem self-evident—the conclusions of simple logic, as they might say. Secularism hasn't had to explain itself for several generations and has become as muddled as religion was when it was simply dominant. Religion, on the other hand, may be becoming more aware of the ideological nature of secular assumptions.

Yet we do not divide neatly into religious and secular populations. We are in some sense amphibious creatures. And I will be showing that our universities have something of this same character. They have never been as thoroughly secularized as we may think. So while there have been other books that counsel mutual tolerance along parallel religious and secular tracks, I will suggest greater interpenetration.[13] We will try not to take the secular university for granted as some religious apologists have done.[14]

The history of the secularization of American universities has been well described and the historians do not reveal a deep laid secularist campaign. Laurence Veysey found several motives inspiring the late-nineteenth-century reformers, involving American ideals of service, German ideals of pure research, and English ones of liberal culture. It would be an exaggeration to think that the sleepy colleges they supplanted, which boasted of promoting mental discipline, had really put their religious views to intellectual or very practical use. Almost none of the academic reformers were "militant skeptics," and Veysey remarks on a "mood of generous, uplifting ethical affirmation." But an ingrained

13. See especially George M. Marsden, *The Outrageous Idea of Christian Scholarship* (New York: Oxford University Press, 1997).
14. D. G. Hart, *The University Gets Religion: Religious Studies in American Higher Education* (Baltimore: Johns Hopkins University Press, 1999), takes the secularity of universities for granted and concludes that religion is better served by staying clear of them. Hart illustrates this from the fortunes of religious studies programs. The position is well maintained within Hart's assumptions, and I will not have to address it in order to make my very different argument. For one thing, I am not talking about the study of religion per se.

religious perspective would give way to a mere interest in religion. Indeed, for themselves and their students, humanists "made a religion out of civilization." At the same time, "the closing years of the nineteenth century saw the rhetorical allegiance to science by professors in most of the disciplines reach giddy heights." Beyond that, there were personal conflicts over academic freedom that created the institutional momentum behind secularization.[15]

By 1910, however, universities were expanding so uncontrollably that "neither the Christian religion in any of its varieties, nor positive science, nor humane culture proved self-evidently capable of making sense out of the entire range of knowledge and opinion."[16] Administrators and students overwhelmed the hopes of faculty and reformers to offer that direction. By now we can see that the "service" impulse has burgeoned into professional education, which is not expected to offer intellectual depth. Meanwhile, research has seemingly imploded into its own black hole, while liberal culture is also disappearing in clouds of self-doubt.

George Marsden added a part of this history which others had missed—that paradoxically it was largely Protestant liberal academics that brought about the secularization of university education. By relentless opposition to their fundamentalist and Catholic competitors, these Protestants encouraged the *definition* of religion as "sectarianism." So ironically, they fostered the now-familiar idea that religion is the enemy of tolerance. The crowning irony is that their efforts helped create our current academic "establishment" of religious nonbelief. For accreditation bodies and government funding agencies have completed the process by ruling against religious perspectives in favor of naturalistic ones, which they mistake for rationality per se.[17]

Yet there were undeniably academics who tried to invent a functional replacement for a religion they thought had no future. The most

---

15. Laurence R. Veysey, *The Emergence of the American University* (Chicago: University of Chicago, 1965), 13, 80, 173, 203–205, 384–418.

16. Ibid., 311.

17. Marsden, *Soul of the American University*. On rationality, see Alasdair MacIntyre, *Whose Justice? Which Rationality?* (Notre Dame: University of Notre Dame, 1988). On Protestantism as a secularizing force, see my *The Secularization of Early Modern England*.

prominent was Charles Eliot Norton of Harvard, whom James Turner credits with the invention of "Western Civilization."

> The introduction into the curriculum of the fine arts and an expansive poetry; the insistence on the practicality, the relevance to daily life, of the liberal culture defined around these new subjects; the replacement, through this culture, of ebbing religiosity with a new secular spirituality coaxed from art and literature; the setting up of these new humanities as a counterweight to American materialism; the use of the humanities to expand the sympathies of students beyond their own class and community, their own time and place; the invention of the idea of Western civilization to provide a matrix for such cosmopolitan sympathies—no American teacher had ever attempted, much less completed, so astonishing a work.[18]

Historian Julie Reuben has gone further, tracing the thoroughgoing "marginalization of morality" in the twentieth-century university. She detected more evidence of conscious efforts to eliminate religious elements, and more belief that science could replace them. Among the universities in her story are three that were pointedly founded with no provision made for a religious presence—Cornell (1865), Johns Hopkins (1876), and Stanford (1891) —and that soon became leaders. In her retelling, the exclusion of religion was a long process: at first it was treated essentially as ethics; then it was made scientific by comparative study, or by postulating its evolutionary or functional core; by relegating it to extracurricular status; by outsourcing it to denominational chaplains; by trusting to faculty role models, then advisers, for moral formation; and finally admission was restricted to students who would bring decent manners with them from home. Nevertheless, her account shows how nonconfrontational this erosion was. In 1912 the religious tone was caught in one historian's hope that universities would foster "an enlightened public opinion and to take a guiding part in public affairs; men who, speaking above the strife of tongues, can say with authority which commands attention: 'This is the way, walk ye in it.' "[19]

As an aside to these histories, Douglas Sloan observes that the no-

---

18. Turner, *Liberal Education of Charles Eliot Norton*, 388.
19. Reuben, *Making of the Modern University*, 4–5, 94–96, 105, 118, 125, 131, 167, 246–262, 166.

table theological renaissance of 1925–1950 in Europe and America, confusingly called "neo-orthodoxy" (and including thinkers I will be quoting), made almost no mark on American universities. Despite its engagement with the existentialism so popular at the time, the secularism of the 1950s could relegate it to the seminaries.[20] The vision at that time was of modernization of the world's institutions, and modernism in the arts, and this progressive prospect did not include religion.

The 1960s, however, would shake the university's self-confidence. Student rebels were attacking not the university's religion but its pretensions to democratic morality and rationalism. It was a time of comprehensive threats to university administration and curricula. A relativizing history of science, feminist perspectives, and a "postmodernist" approach to popular and ethnic cultures found ineffective resistance. The list could go on. The postmodernist insistence that modern rationalism was not self-evident finally registered with students. After the class final, they would feel free to think what they liked. Postmodernism was the greater threat for having come from *within* the academy.

In all of this upheaval, however, the one boundary that the university knew could be defended was that against religious perspectives. While there might be kind words for an aesthetic "spirituality," the academic mood toward public religion continued to sour. This was not necessarily at leading institutions so much as at those which felt pressed to buttress their insecurity by boundary maintenance.

The mention of cultural democracy brings us to the last point of this chapter, which is the decline of argument and the rise of intellectual fashion. Arguments, remember, depend on settled reference points you can hold your opponent to. Proving something means appealing to your opponents' assumptions and showing that logical consistency requires them to accept your conclusions, based on some agreed evidence.

These days we talk about something different: "the marketplace of ideas." It's an apt metaphor for our situation, and even for the university. Back in 1900 it was actually possible to keep up with the intellec-

20. Douglas Sloane, *Faith and Knowledge: Mainline Protestantism and American Higher Education* (Louisville: Westminster John Knox, 1994), x, 57.

tual debates in very wide fields. There were just a few scholarly journals to read. Writers deployed their proofs, and nobody felt free to ignore the published results of this scholarship. Things are different now. So much is published that nobody can keep up with more than their sub-specialty.

This encourages the current talk about tolerance and diversity. We used to talk about truth, but now we talk about tolerance. They're not incompatible. Rationalism promoted tolerance and relativism as necessary means in the search for a many-sided truth. But as truth seems to recede into the distance, tolerance and relativism cease to be means and become ends in themselves. We see this in the widespread suspicion of people who insist on the word "truth" and are therefore suspected of being bigots of some kind.

Tolerance and relativism were once used to cast doubt on religious assertions. But they can work on rationalist ones as well. The general public could well find this a congenial situation, when no one can tell them what to think. In a cultural democracy everybody has a vote in philosophy as well as in politics. It may produce an incoherent world, one in which our high-tech hospitals are the main prayer centers, or where movie special-effects technology is used to produce religious experience. One can even imagine a scenario in which science is prized primarily as a servant of religious ends, having no intrinsic ends of its own.

We need not think of fashion as something foisted on the university by the public. One would think that historians, of all people, would resist a loss of traditional views. But the American Historical Association announces a theme for each of its annual convention ahead of time, setting the historical style, as it were. Several years ago the president of the association polled prominent historians about these conventions, and the most common complaint was that they were too "trendy." That year the theme was "Frontiers and Empires," part of the current fashion for global themes—the "flavor of the month," as we say. Graduate students especially are eager for the new "buzzword" that will have its "fifteen minutes of fame." When you see these once-fashionable words later—like *conjuncture, mentalité, longue durée*—they seem a little dowdy. But "that was then, this is now," we think, in still another of our fashion-conscious phrases.

Postmodernism itself might serve as an example of such academic fashion. It didn't begin as a fashion, but rather as a true paradigm shift. Paradigm shifts are not popular, or not at first. If your field were hit by a paradigm shift, it would call all your training and your previous career into question. Paradigm shifts are not caused by boredom and restlessness, like fashions. They are caused by wrenchingly new perspectives. The various things that went under the heading of postmodernism highlighted things we hadn't noticed before.

But it is different when people begin posturing as postmodernists, new historicists, deconstructionists, and so forth, because they need a brand name in the marketplace. The names replace each other in an endless succession of fashions, which suggests that academics are part of the entertainment world. Eventually "paradigm shift" makes it to TV commercials. It reminds us that fashions tend toward absurdity and exaggeration, and the American public may see some of that in its universities.

I've been suggesting that the secular university was a flawed concept from the beginning. At the beginning, it was expected to offer information and skills and also to answer some more searching questions about life. It has done the former. But we have learned that it can't translate information into action. If we ever hoped it would give us guidance, we have dropped that notion by now.

When giving this chapter as a talk, I was challenged by someone who had taken a course that he said did a wonderfully fair and complete job on the bioethics questions that are among our most troubling today. He thought the course gave full attention to the concept of the human, which creates great problems for the kind of naturalism that universities tend to assume. He showed me the course syllabus, which challenged my insinuation of the university's failure. I still had two concerns. First, only 25 students took the course, in a university of 45,000 students who would all have profited from it. Most of those never heard of the course, and might resist anything they thought would try to tell them what to think. Second, the teacher would probably have recoiled from the suggestion that students would come to firm conclusions as opposed to recognizing the complexity of the issues. Students who closed their minds around some truth about the issues would probably be graded down. They would be accused of violating the fact/value dichotomy that we will discuss in chapter 3.

What happens after students leave our most thoughtful courses and try to put their knowledge to work? A century ago colleges recognized the need to connect knowledge and decision. One thinks back to the requirement of chapel attendance. One can imagine students meditating over matters of decision or the future direction of their research. Why does that sound silly now? Is it because nowhere in our education do we hear anything about prayer? Our ideas on the subject are the childish ones we never developed for lack of a challenge to do so.

When academics think of religion they may assume that it makes only assertions, not arguments. They may not realize how much religion remains embedded in our current thinking. We can't even discuss the concepts of wealth, justice, sanity, truth, the human, and the humane without finding their irreducibly religious dimensions. For all of these involve the question of what human life is all about, of what would be optimal for humanity. Naturalism is silent on these subjects. A century ago it seemed reasonable to restrict the university to questions we could answer definitively, to everyone's satisfaction. We are now finding that this leaves out too much.

The ground rules of scholarship hardly allow an integration of scholarship and decision. Knowledge and faith, information and decision, meet within a person, not within an argument. But we could come much closer if we gave up the artificial constraints imposed by legal secularism.

David Kirp, after exploring the market-driven trends in higher education, had to admit that "incoherence about what knowledge matters most goes well beyond the curriculum; it has become pervasive in higher education." He quotes Clark Kerr, former president of the California university system, who said in 2001 that universities have "no great visions to lure them on, only the need for survival" common to all institutions.[21]

---

21. Kirp, *Shakespeare, Einstein, and the Bottom Line*, 259.

In short, we seem to have gone through secularism and come out the other side. Postsecularism represents a more level playing field, but the games we play are pretty chaotic. Many new voices are being heard, but some old ones are still silenced by the long-standing ban on Western religion. But fashion itself may allow an opening in that direction, and I hope to explore some opportunities that could offer the erstwhile secular university. It would not need to be so dismissive and so ineffective, and a wider society could take a renewed interest.

David Brooks's *Bobos in Paradise* describes the foibles of our new elites, the products of our modern universities. Brooks is thankful to be part of the class he describes, but at the end he makes a telling point. This group of the educated and prosperous, descended from the bohemian radicals on one side and bourgeois strivers on the other, don't really seem like leaders. Nobody is going to call them "the greatest generation," as Tom Brokaw termed a bunch of high school dropouts. So far they haven't shown the courage, faith, or grit that was necessary to meet the severe trials of sixty or seventy years ago. When we are tested in the future, it is not to be expected that our leadership will come from the higher reaches of our universities. Their "complacency," as Brooks calls it, is of a piece with their tolerance, detachment, and self-absorption.

If our universities are to become more than professional schools, their rationalism needs to be in dialogue with other "traditions of inquiry." For the most important matters in life include such matters as hope, depression, trust, purpose, and wisdom. If secularism purges such concerns from the curriculum for lack of a way to address them, the public may conclude that the football team really is the most important part of the university. But if they are taken up, we will find ourselves using terms that seem to belong in a religious discourse. We have dodged this issue by saying that true, good, just, are all political, meaning that they can't be discussed but only voted on. But in fact they could be discussed if our discussions were to recognize a dimension of ultimacy. It will do wonders in drawing attention and respect to our universities. And it ought to make religion itself a less frivolous thing than it has become.

2

TROUBLE DEFINING THE HUMAN

If there is one thing that should raise the question of the secular university's irrelevance, it might especially be in the failure to justify or even make sense of the concept of the human. Do we define the human as any more than the species *Homo sapiens*? Was Darwin justified in rubbing out the line between humans and other life-forms? Does the fact that we are made of hydrocarbons mean that is all we are? Or is there something irreducible in the concept of the human, something that may involve religious terms?

A lot is at stake here. If universities fail to make sense of human difference, how can they explain the law school, which implies our transcendence as moral ends? Or psychology programs, serving notions of sanity? Or the business school, which ought to be promoting well-being or "wealth"? Or fine arts, or liberal arts and humanities, or public administration, or health and human services? All of professional education, which absorbs the great majority of students today, depends on some particular understanding, even some ideal, of the human. So the concept of the human is constantly at issue. It is unfashionable views of the human which are at issue in the rejection of traditional standards in law, literature, or the assessment of "life." Such rejection is not without its passion, along with its confusion.

Even science, at the very heart of our cultural authority, makes no sense outside of the context of the human. Science is a human practice, embodying human intellectual categories, serving human purposes, having no purposes of its own. That is, science is not the disembodied product of some logic or evolution within matter; scientists choose what they judge to be promising subjects, and we decide how to apply their knowledge. This is ironic, since science may be taken to refute the human distinction. It seems to be committed to conceptual reduction of the human to lower levels of analysis. But in fact, science's very existence *proves* human transcendence, as philosophers like William James and theologians like Emil Brunner have remarked.[1]

It is worth noting that scientists themselves clearly accept the human difference whenever they actually restrict their research for moral reasons. Though indignant at the idea of public curbs on science, they routinely put limits on themselves and each other. For most scientists are as horrified as anyone at the excesses of, for example, Nazi science. They may claim that it was not really science at all. But it is not a lack of experimental rigor they are objecting to as much as the unrestrained use of *Homo sapiens*, whose humanity is being ignored. Thus scientists are responding to ideas they may have learned as religious taboos and have never found an independent basis for. Science itself didn't teach them that humans shouldn't be treated as things. Or perhaps we have here an instance of the inadequacy of the fact/value dichotomy, which we will address in the next chapter.

We are so used to thinking of "humanism" and religion as rivals that we may not have noticed that the cultural struggle now is between some obscure kind of humanism on the one hand and naturalism on the other. When American universities became officially secular, a century ago, the problem of defining the human was not foreseen. Much of a traditional Christian intellectual culture was taken for granted. Mistaking their habits of thinking for rationality itself, those founders thought religion was redundant and could be ignored without loss of substance. It has taken a century to discover the intellectual void that results when religious categories are systematically rejected wherever they are discovered. Thoughtful commentators now speak of "secular inhumanism."

---

1. Hans Joas, *The Genesis of Values* (Chicago: University of Chicago Press, 2000), 38; Emil Brunner, *The Christian Doctrine of Creation and Redemption* (Philadelphia: Westminster, 1952), 84.

We also see the phrase "posthuman" given currency in such works as Francis Fukuyama's *Our Posthuman Future: Consequences of the Biotechnology Revolution* (2002). He foresees a time when we can create human hybrids and will have to puzzle over any rights they may have as against our own. Fukuyama does acknowledge religious positions as an alternative to his own Aristotelian position on conceiving the human difference, but he brushes past them. So we may need to point out the additional strengths in a religious, and most familiarly a Christian, position.

First, though, we should note how easily scientists become confused on this subject. The late Stephen Jay Gould, even while trying to address religious readers, betrayed assumptions about the human that his naturalistic assumptions could not accommodate. In *Rocks of Ages* (1999) he emphasized that humans are simply part of nature and, as such, are no more special than a snail. "Nature," he says, is "sublimely indifferent" toward humankind, and more colloquially, "Nature doesn't give a damn about us."[2] Note that this is by a man who clearly thought that "nature" was all there is.

Yet humans are not indifferent to humans, so are they still part of nature? Obviously Gould somehow believes that humans have transcended whatever he means by nature. Elsewhere he says that "Nature is amoral," in the midst of a discussion of our moral duties.[3] Journalists follow suit: The *New Yorker* for 10 December 2001 (p. 84) offers that "ethics are made by humans, not found in the world." So what all does the world consist of? It seems that we are in the world but not of it. As the Bard put it, "There are more things in heaven and earth than are dreamt of in your philosophy."

We all fall into Gould's habit of thinking that we are not really part of "the universe" but have dropped in from another dimension. It is our awkward way of registering that the human is mysterious. This sense is surely behind the attempt of religious conservatives to have the

---

2. Stephen Jay Gould, *Rocks of Ages: Science and Religion in the Fullness of Life* (New York: Ballantine, 1999), 177–178, 195, 202.
3. Ibid., 195.

concept of creation recognized within science. But what we might be doing instead is incorporating science within an intellectual framework that is religiously suggestive (see chapter 6).

To say that "nature is all there is" doesn't tell us anything so long as we are still learning all that nature might mean. It suggests a rush to judgment, a metaphysical dictate rather than a scientific discovery. This naturalistic ideology has grown careless because it is so rarely challenged.

In his classic *Sources of the Self: The Making of the Modern Identity*, philosopher Charles Taylor reminds us that the appearance of human beings actually created new realities in the universe. However we appeared, an adequate account of reality now has to include concepts of the human and its corollaries, which cannot be conceptually reduced or subsumed in the usual naturalistic terms.

> Human science can no longer be couched in the terms of physics. Our value terms purport to give us insight into what it is to live in the universe as a human being, and this is a quite different matter from that which physical science claims to reveal and explain. This reality is, of course, dependent on us, in the sense that a condition for its existence is our existence. But once granted that we exist, it is no more a subjective projection than what physics deals with. . . . What is real is what you have to deal with, what won't go away just because it doesn't fit with your prejudices.[4]

In short, the words we must use to describe human qualities and concerns refer to primary realities, things as real as hydrocarbon.

It is common to say that humans are part of nature, as if that somehow reduces us. But to say that humans are part of nature also says something about *nature*. What it says is that a lot of terms that we use of humans and only of humans reveal something as real about the universe as atoms or galaxies. (Philosopher Martin Heidegger was saying something like this in grounding his analysis of Being in human being, and not meaning simply *Homo sapiens*.[5]) These terms are the corollaries

4. Charles Taylor, *Sources of the Self: The Making of the Modern Identity* (Cambridge, MA: Harvard University Press, 1989), 59.
5. See George Steiner, *Martin Heidegger* (New York: Penguin, 1980), 107.

of the concept of the human, like trust, responsibility, hope, justice, science, purpose, creativity. And they haven't been reduced to a lower conceptual, that is, a more basic scientific, level. Linguistic philosophers hold that words are fundamental elements in our lifeworld, since we don't have direct access to things-in-themselves. These personalist terms cannot be fully replaced by physicalist ones. The efforts that have been made seem unconvincing; there is always a remainder of meaning. Sociobiologists were the latest to attempt such reductions, but they were greeted with general skepticism, having largely been refuted in advance by the arguments against utilitarianism.

The question about the human is not exhausted by telling us where our bodies came from, or even about where human consciousness comes from. It is about the meanings we can give to the human, what an ideal of humanity might be, or what we could aim at. These are not questions one asks about chimpanzees, let alone cabbages.

Those corollaries of the human are words that we *must* use of human life, but that we *cannot* use of other animals. Justice, for example, we don't use in relation to other animals; what we call animal rights are not the rights animals recognize with respect to each other, but only govern humans. Like the other terms, it defies deconstruction, and like them it is obviously part of various religious discourses.

It is not fruitful to deal with this issue by looking for a level of reality that is real per se. Things at each of the analytical levels of being (represented roughly by the different sciences, like economics, sociology, psychology, physiology, cell science, biochemistry, physics) are "real to each other."[6] So attempts to claim that justice is "merely, nothing but, just, simply, basically" something else always fail to exhaust its meaning. Wealth, in the sense of well-being, refers to the optimal for humans. Sanity, truth, the humane, all imply optimal states of our nature and only our nature. If one can't reduce these concepts (to survival value, for instance), then they have established the only kind of "reality" philosophers recognize, that is, irreducibility. Fukuyama himself

---

6. William Wimsatt, "Reductionism, Levels of Organization, and the Mind-Body Problem," in *Consciousness and the Brain*, ed. Gordon G. Globus, Grover Maxwell, and Irwin Savodnik (New York: Plenum, 1976), 205–267.

variously mentions justice, politics, and science itself as witnessing to the irreducibly human.[7]

Fukuyama prefers an Aristotelian language in dealing with the human difference, because so many readers are conditioned to reject anything that sounds religious. Aristotle grounded his understanding of the human in natural norms, empirically. That served Aristotle's purpose of showing that human nature transcends our cultural differences as well as our biological difference from other animals. Later philosophers tried other ways to establish the human difference. Fukuyama observes that while Kant could not prove the free will that was his defining characteristic of the human, he presented it as "a necessary postulate" of our reason. While Fukuyama thinks that a "hard-bitten empirical scientist" would hardly accept that, such a scientist would have intellectual difficulties of his own in accounting for humane concepts.[8] And while the utilitarian arguments for morality which attract naturalistic philosophers might work for the group, they don't work for the individual.

There are those who continue the Kantian tradition in pointing out the strangeness of creatures who find themselves at odds with their natural desires, and who recognize obligations that bring them a negative benefit—the essence of Kant's moral situation.[9] It is probably not incidental that such arguments are promoted by scholars with a religious identification, like Charles Taylor, Christian Smith, and George Mavrodes. It has been noted that these arguments are absent from textbooks in the social sciences.[10] Such textbooks might prefer a secular understanding of the human like Kant's "necessary postulate," which falls short of a definition.

---

7. Francis Fukuyama, *Our Posthuman Future: Consequences of the Biotechnology Revolution* (New York: Picador, 2002), 165, 186.

8. Ibid., 12–13, 151.

9. Taylor, *Sources of the Self*, 4; Christian Smith, *Moral, Believing Animals: Human Personhood and Culture* (New York: Oxford University Press, 2003), 8; George I. Mavrodes, "Religion and the Queerness of Morality," in *Rationality, Religious Belief, and Moral Commitment*, ed. Robert Audi and William Wainwright (Ithaca: Cornell University Press, 1986), 213–226.

10. Smith, *Moral, Believing Animals*, 17.

For example, to quote *The Encyclopedia of Philosophy* on the subject of human rights:

> The concept of human rights presupposes a standard below which it is intolerable that a human being should fall—not just in the way that cruelty to an animal is not to be tolerated but, rather, that human deprivations affront some ideal conception of what a human life ought to be like, a conception of human excellence.[11]

This is just a free-floating idea or belief, apparently. Political philosopher John Rawls admits as much in saying that we must (*sic*) accept the fiction of responsibility even if it is not rationally justified.[12] So universities muddle through with a big mystery at their center: a mystery in the shape of religion.

Before considering the contribution that a religious discourse could make to this, we might glance at the current animal rights debate. It further reveals the inability of academic naturalism to ignore the human distinction. The very titles of the books show this, like Tom Regan and Peter Singer's *Animal Rights and Human Obligations*. Singer embarks on one of those searches to find an empirical characteristic that sets humans apart (the only animals who . . .). He concludes that there is no "actual" or "concrete difference" for the "moral gulf which is commonly thought to separate animals and humans": "There seems to be no relevant characteristic that human infants possess that adult mammals do not have to the same or a higher degree."[13]

The difference that Singer is seeking is going to be not a "concrete" (i.e., biological) difference but a moral one, and it is already enshrined in his title. His own animal rights project depends on a human differ-

11. *The Encyclopedia of Philosophy*, ed. Paul Edwards (New York: Macmillan and Free Press, 1967), 7:199.
12. See *Routledge Encyclopedia of Philosophy*, ed. Edward Craig (New York: Routledge, 1998), 4:522.
13. Tom Regan and Peter Singer, eds., *Animal Rights and Human Obligations*, 2d ed. (Englewood Cliffs, NJ: Prentice-Hall, 1989), 80–82.

ence that is at least as significant as tool-using, tool-making or sign-using. Only humans feel the moral obligation in his title. So the animal rights movement itself is evidence for the gulf between animals and humans that Singer says does not exist.

The difference is apparently too big to see. Singer began his chapter, "All Animals are Equal," by asserting that we are all equal in a moral sense. But of course we are not equal in *having* this moral sense. Animals are not having parallel concerns about respecting our rights. If Singer truly followed Darwin's view that species flowed into each other without clear distinctions, there could be nothing "wrong" with our ravaging other animals for food or simply to extinguish their gene stream.

Singer holds that "equality is a moral ideal, not a simple matter of fact."[14] But if we can't wish such moral distinctions away, then they are what we call matters of fact. Morals "exist" in humans or Singer could not appeal to them and would have no audience. If he can't retitle the book *Human Rights and Animal Obligations*, it means that all animals are not equal.

Singer's coeditor, Tom Regan, argues the human/nonhuman distinction away by saying that equal respect for animals rests on their having the same "experience of life" as we do.[15] He thinks they may well share a similar experience of pain, and perhaps even of consciousness. But if humans are dominated by concepts such as evil, justice, truth, and the like, then we do not have the same experience of life as other animals. This doesn't end the discussion of how we should treat animals. It only reminds us that we will not be cooperating with a like concern among them.

Other secularist thinkers betray similar commitments to the human distinction. Marxists might argue that our humanity is actually created by social conditions, but they cannot help talking of the dehumanizing effects of modern life or of our alienation from our true selves.[16] Attempts like Timothy H. Goldsmith's to find "the biological roots of human nature" write promissory notes backed by an evolutionary faith in materialist determinism. But that book never gets "higher" in its

---

14. Ibid., 77.
15. Ibid., 111–113.
16. Roger Trigg, *Ideas of Human Nature* (Oxford: Basil Blackwell, 1988), 107.

discussions of human thought and culture than comments on sexual reproduction. The real test of such a project would be if he could present a convincing sociobiological explanation of sociobiology itself. In writing the book, Goldsmith was responding to ethical concerns that his philosophy would find no place for.

Neuroscientists who assert that all mental processes are physical matters don't actually believe that their own "thoughts" are only the latest products of eons of evolutionary change. They think they are developing a science of true statements, not simply registering the mental formulations favored by some survival value. Of course, purposes and intentions may register something in the brain that is physically measurable, but those scientists' purposes still transcend anything merely mechanical. If their writings put "self," "mind," "soul" in quotation marks, we may take it as an admission that their scientific discourse couldn't accommodate such difficult concepts and may never do so. It wouldn't mean these concepts were unreal, except for those with an absolute faith in physicalist reductions.

But what does it mean, and what difference would it make, to say that the language of the human is more at home in a religious discourse? The difference is that it would reopen our universities to a wider philosophical and cultural heritage.

The terms we use to describe human affairs are not comfortable within a language of naturalism. We have not seriously attempted their translation into that language since B. F. Skinner gave it up a half century ago. When we say that "human" is a religious term, we mean that it has coherent meanings in a religious discourse. It relates grammatically to other concepts like "purpose," "creation," "evil," "equality," "concern," "beauty," and "wealth, which will bog down any naturalistic analysis. All these terms have recognized uses within religious discourse.[17] If we want to use them at all (and clearly we must), it will be hard to avoid religious associations. If universities rule out all such discussions as soon as they recognize them as religious (involving even

17. See Alvin Plantinga, *Warranted Christian Belief* (New York: Oxford University Press, 2000), for an extensive exposition of the coherence of one religious tradition.

Plato, for instance), then serious discussion will migrate to some other venue.

Of course we will need to refine this religious discourse. It is seriously rusty from disuse. But the academy needs to learn to speak theologically. This undoubtedly sounds alarming, but we've been doing it all along, on a primitive and unconscious level. Meanwhile, we can continue the parallel attempt to speak of religions naturalistically, in the terms of psychology, sociology or evolutionary biology. Those sciences can doubtless show that much religious *behavior* can be explained in those terms. Still, the *concepts* of religion and of the human will survive, witnessing to an ultimacy that we can't ignore.

Long ago, and again recently, Christian philosophers have been in serious dialogue with Aristotle in discussing these matters. But they are typically reluctant to do without some concept of creation, which some believe would complete his thinking. Optimal human states imply purposes, intentions, and ultimately some notion of creation, which take one beyond Aristotle's empiricism. For the semantics of "human" suggests something like purpose.

When Thomas Jefferson wrote that all men are *created* equal, he could still assume creation and purpose. Darwin changed all that. But we cannot say that all men have *evolved* equally. So we have had to proceed with our analysis of politics, society, and economics without agreement on final principles.

For a time after Darwin, creation was simply not an issue within science. Many physicists were satisfied to consider the universe "eternal." But cosmology has stumbled onto something like creation again, in the notion of a Big Bang. This has even acquired a contingent character in the form of the so-called Anthropic Coincidences. In other words, we can recognize that creation didn't just happen, but happened in a particular way. We are talking here of the thirty-odd incredibly fine-tuned constants within our universe which together made the appearance of intelligent life not just possible but apparently foreordained, from the moment of the origin. Our existence, or something like us, was no accident. Scientists shake their heads in wonder, or snort in disbelief, depending on their personal disposition and not on their different insight. For there is no way to really talk about this amazing discovery. No way within science, that is. Religious discourse, on the other hand, does accommodate creation-talk, in speaking of the personal and of purpose. And such talk is subject to critical reflection of the sort that belongs in universities.

As secularization was first setting in, philosophers preserved a sense of the human within natural law doctrine. Jefferson knew something of this discussion. Even after the decline of those doctrines, various philosophical schools tried to treat personality and culture as primary realities, challenging simple physicalism. Rudolf Hermann Lotze and others in the late nineteenth century developed "philosophies of spirit" in opposition to the materialism of their times. Soren Kierkegaard inspired a number of philosophers of "personal being," in opposition to Idealism. Wilhelm Dilthey pioneered the philosophies of history and of culture that stand behind the narrative theories developing today. And Martin Heidegger inspired philosophies of existence, against a developing positivism. He pointed out how *human* being, which *experiences* time, is different from those forms of being that only *persist* in time. These schools of thought, however, have never captured the public mind. The public, it seems, still assumes we are perfecting a physicalist philosophy-cum-science. One detects this hope in the dubious assurances that neuroscience will crack the mystery of consciousness.

Where in the university today could we face the overwhelming question of human significance, without some dismissive gesture? What answers are ruled out in advance by a secularism that professes to be agnostic? And shouldn't such a dismissal be seen as a sign of timidity rather than of assurance? Could we not have a respectful debate that admitted religious voices?

One of the favorite ways that existentialist philosophers tried to argue the primacy of human concerns was to ask how death forces the ultimate issue of what our lives are for. Mortality raises the question of whether you are wasting the one lifetime you'll ever have. Such debates end at the point at which one's faith is revealed. That could be a proper use of the university's attention, even though it might not be universally compelling. Since faith is inevitably involved in completing our intellectual pilgrimage, the university might acknowledge that fact.

Almost every day we are asked to consider how to assess human lives. What is a life worth, in terms of liability costs or civil torts? Or in terms of victim restitution, wartime casualty counts, capital punishment? Beyond this, our vague ideas of the human underlie disagreements on sex education, city planning, human rights, poverty programs, biomedical hybrids, criminal punishment, art galleries, public relations, health administration, general education requirements, conservation, to name a few. The university would get more attention if it could invite a wider range of voices into discussions of the subject.

Times of threat to humanity, like the world wars of the last century, have forced the issue of the human upon philosophers in an urgent form. Certainly the threat of officially atheistic communism did so. Polish philosopher Leszek Kolakowski wrestled with such problems philosophically before recognizing them as fundamentally theological. He came to believe that the human distinction disappears along with the disappearance of the sacred: "With the disappearance of the sacred, which imposed limits to the perfection that could be attained by the profane, arises one of the most dangerous illusions of our civilization—the illusion that there are no limits to the changes that human life can undergo."[18] That is, to preserve respect for our humanity there must be limits that we might not be able to "explain": that is sacred limits. As an observer of the communist experiment, Kolakowski saw respect for the human disappearing, as frightful demands were made on hapless populations. Secular totalitarianism acknowledged no limits—no "taboos," as he puts it—on their treatment of human persons. The human implies limits—he calls them "sacred limits"—on our treatment of each other.

Further, Kolakowski notes that the "sense [of the human] can come only from the sacred; it cannot be produced by empirical research."[19] He means that the human difference is not something one finds in a search for a defining difference between *Homo sapiens* and other species. All those efforts to argue that we are the only animals that (whatever) represent a misguided attempt to make it an empirical rather than a hermeneutical search. Hermeneutical searches seek to discover inescap-

18. Leszek Kolakowski, *Modernity on Endless Trial* (Chicago: University of Chicago Press, 1990), 72–73.
19. Ibid.

able meanings rather than constituent elements. And some things find their reality in those meanings.

An empirical search for the human essence would be entangled with the issue of whether *Homo sapiens* has changed over time. Whether or not this would affect an Aristotelian view of human nature, it need not affect a religious one. Christianity, for instance, does not teach that we always successfully embody a truly human life. "Sin" is the word for that which distances us from our true nature. It is a hard concept to ignore. Fukuyama acknowledges something of the sort by having separate chapters on human nature and human dignity, trying to bring the concept within the scope of the academy.

Terminology like this will initially be startling within our secularist universities. It is incommensurable with the long drift toward naturalism. Philosopher Alasdair MacIntyre takes up just this problem of incommensurable outlooks. He holds that such competitions are won by those views that can include their rivals, but cannot themselves be so included.[20] Sociologist Christian Smith offers one such argument, asserting that his "narrative" of "the moral, believing animal" contains the rationalists' "rational-choice" model of humanity but cannot itself be contained in the latter.[21] Such projects are known as efforts to "outnarrate" your opponent.

I have asserted that there are many terms that even the secular university cannot do without, like "truth," "freedom," "sanity," "responsibility," and "purpose," that are more comfortable within various religious discourses. Naturalistic discourse only offers the promise of someday making sense. Its efforts to include the concept as well as the substance of religion within its sociological or psychological or sociobiological categories have not ended in success. Even Nietzsche and Foucault, who sought to reduce the human to power and desire, couldn't help pressing the *truth* of their views, and presumably they wanted their publications to have some humane effect. Meanwhile, religious discourse has always felt it can make sense of naturalism. It is at no loss to offer personalist explanations of science. Indeed, the academic his-

20. Alasdair MacIntyre, *Three Rival Versions of Moral Enquiry* (Notre Dame: University of Notre Dame Press, 1990), 81.

21. Smith, *Moral, Believing Animals*, 158.

tory of science regularly deals in religious explanations of both the encouragement of science and the cultural resistance to it.

As an example of what professors and students who want to boast of an education should be made to consider, I suggest Walker Percy's essay "Is a Theory of Man Possible?"[22] As a medical doctor Percy was dissatisfied with the classical soul/body model of earlier philosophy and theology. But as a Christian humanist and novelist he was also unconvinced by the organismic, behaviorist model of Darwinian naturalism. He saw weighty objections to both views. But it seemed to him that C. S. Peirce and semiotics offered an alternative theory that took the human difference seriously and began to explain it. Humanity's very sudden acquisition of language and the growth spurt that resulted drew attention to the creative effect of that gift. For language does not appear to be the *result* of increased brain size, consciousness, self, world-formation, or the fact that humanity is not comfortable in its native environment. Rather, Percy wanted to explore the possibility that language or symbolization was the *cause* of these phenomena. This is not a theory that sets science and theology in opposition; rather, it has the potential to relate them in mutual respect. Finding personality and purpose in the universe—beginning from ourselves—is suggestive of religion, whatever it may require of theological formulations. In the beginning was the Word.

With regard to considerations of the human, religion has recently gained a powerful ally within the academy in the rediscovery of narrative. It is becoming apparent that narrative is not just a descriptive method but also a method of inquiry. The university has long operated as if analysis, taking things apart to understand them, was the only intellectual method. That was the way of science, after all. But philosophers since Heidegger have realized that this doesn't work so well when discussing human Being. We have already noted that the thing that makes humans distinctive is that we experience time. Our "bodies" may only persist in time, like objects, and they will still benefit from medical analysis. But if we have questions about human motives, action,

22. Walker Percy, *Signposts in a Strange Land* (New York: Picador, 1991), 111–129.

thinking, hopes, the answers will come through considering our narratives.

This has been a dramatic reversal. In the 1960s there was some effort to turn academic history itself into a social science, using analytical methods. The goal would have been the discovery of laws of social behavior under determinist assumptions. That proved a dead end and was given up.[23] And it is not only historians who now accept the primacy of narrative and thereby assume human freedom. The same direction can be seen within the social sciences themselves, which have begun recounting stories, and not just producing graphs and scatter diagrams. Psychotherapy has been forced to recognize itself as a humanistic philosophy, using narrative and hermeneutic approaches. As an applied philosophy of life, it finds itself in a very different relationship to religion than Freud assumed. Spirituality now seems more formidable territory, and not something to be dismissed out of hand.[24] Finally, physicians too are finding that in applying medical knowledge they need to hear their patients' stories.

Science itself turns out to be a narrative. What used to pass for a history of science mostly connected factual dots representing important discoveries. But that is not how science developed. The new history of science, beginning in the 1960s, has shown that discovery is a fully human story. Scientists fought and argued and were mistaken and wasted time and had breakthroughs that had nothing to do with logic. All this had been ignored in the triumphalist histories of science, which thought of it simply as a logical progression. The process of discovery is very different from the logic of confirmation. And the scientific "revolutions" or disruptions that historians now describe often turn out to be the most interesting parts of the story.

Narrative has a special affinity with religion in the West. Unlike other civilizations, the West was long dominated by a sacred text set within a narrative framework. It is not propositional, declarative, epigrammatic, or prophetic so much as historical. And it is the history of

23. Peter Novick, *That Noble Dream: The "Objectivity Question" and the American Historical Profession* (Cambridge: Cambridge University Press, 1988), 392–400, 622–624.
24. Paul Vitz, "Psychology in Recovery," *First Things* 151 (March 2005): 17–21.

humans. So it is no wonder that the main proponents of narrative theories are attuned to religious questions. Heidegger began as a Catholic theology student and associate of Karl Barth, who may be taken as the first narrative theologian. Paul Ricoeur, the major narrative metaphysician, and Michael Polanyi, who brilliantly showed the narrative character of scientific research, had a similar attraction to Christian thought. These figures have recently been joined by famously Christian philosophers like Alasdair MacIntyre, Charles Taylor, John Milbank, and Stanley Hauerwas.

The magic of narrative texts is that they pull us inside, so that we can experience the human in a richer way. If the university more frankly admitted the concept of the human, students might again thrill to the heightened experience, even religious experience, that was once the purpose of literature. We could stop paying professors to dispel its subversive attractions. This would go counter to recent currents, where the secularist humanities have declared war on metanarratives because of their hegemonic power. After all, we can now see that the rejection of narrative is itself part of a narrative.[25]

If the point of the secular university was to eliminate the religious dimension, it will eventually find that it has eliminated the human distinction as well, and be unable to make sense of any of its intellectual or professional disciplines. One might rather hope for a renewal of the great hermeneutic project of exploring the meanings of "human," in the terms of those optimal states, even virtues. In the words of theologian Barth, a sense of God's relation to the creation "does not rest on a worldview, but on a view of man which sees in him the point in the cosmos where the thoughts of its Creator are disclosed."[26] What thoughts? Start with those concepts that we must use about humans but cannot use of other animals. We need to hear what the terms say to us, instead of trying to shush them by deconstruction or reduction. What we hear could be the beginning of a greater realism.

25. Smith, *Moral, Believing Animals*, 65–73, 87–88.
26. Karl Barth, *Church Dogmatics*, III, 2, pp. 18–19.

3

Trouble Maintaining the Fact/ Value Dichotomy

One of the foundations of the secular university, recognized as basic by the 1920s, was the fact/value dichotomy. It held that we are not supposed to be able to derive a value from a fact, or an "ought" from an "is." To do so was thought to commit the "naturalistic fallacy." This supposedly impassible division is widely taken to be a cornerstone of science. But there is now some question about how much validity the principle has. The fact/value dichotomy is now under attack and is seen as a cornerstone of "scientism," which is not so much science as an ideological exaltation of science. Scientism was, however, a major part of twentieth-century secularism. So the fact that the dichotomy is now being questioned by important philosophers weakens a pillar of the secularist university.

If the line between facts and values is blurred, there is less basis for the common view that nature gives us no guidelines and that it is up to humanity to set its own standards. This is the familiar "existentialist" view that humanity must create itself. If one could find openings between fact and value, there may actually be something in the way of a human nature that we would be wise to respect. "Reality" may offer certain ethical constraints, like the natural law philosophers long argued. And of course it is relevant to our theme that natural law, natural rights, and ideas of human nature have been in dialogue with theology for centuries. A well-appointed university, like many in Europe, would have a theology department (not the same thing as "religious studies") that could dialogue with philosophers on such questions.

◦———

Julie Reuben, in *The Making of the Modern University: Intellectual Transformation and the Marginalization of Morality*, has shown the importance of the fact/value distinction to the secularization of the American university. German sociologist Max Weber was the one who popularized the principle as the touchstone of science. At first the dichotomy was resisted, she finds, because professors hoped to have a prophetic role as policy advisers in their areas of expertise. They wanted to derive practical ends from their specialized knowledge. There were efforts to create a naturalistic ethics, by John Dewey for instance, which would have been a scientific colonization of ethics. But by the 1920s scholars began to appreciate the fact that a rigid fact/value distinction freed them from moral scrutiny by administrators and taxpayers. Their work could go on behind a wall separating the two realms. This may have been hard on social scientists, who would forfeit a policy role, but it was the price they paid to be considered scientists. And already in the 1910s those who were left on the wrong side of that wall were calling themselves "humanists" by way of contrast.[1]

Religious scholars at first objected to separating value from fact, thinking that ethics would be ignored once it lost its connection to the most rigorous understandings of reality. But that was when religious thought still enjoyed more respect in the academy and its professors expected to be listened to. By the later twentieth century even religious spokespersons had decided that there might be advantages to the division. Scientists could not tell them they were wrong in their considerations of value. Postmodernists were by then arguing the radical difference of intellectual positions and announcing the end of a rationalism that could judge all claims. So religions could take their places at the table with all those presuppositional positions. It could debate its positions as securely as others, now that everybody was part of a minority.

1. Julie A. Reuben, *The Making of the Modern University: Intellectual Transformation and the Marginalization of Morality* (Chicago: University of Chicago Press, 1996), 2, 145, 174, 188–194, 213.

Some religious scholars, however, resisted the dichotomy. Douglas Sloan, in 1994, questioned the dichotomy, citing those like the philosopher of science Norwood Russell Hanson, who had long insisted that the merest facts are theory-laden. Such philosophers had pointed out that "the methodological assumptions of the disciplines help determine at the outset the nature of the facts themselves" so that "the data are a function of the method used."[2] Thus, scientific conceptualizations should not be considered "reality" unless one simply defined them as such. Sloan's book was published by a religious press, however, and was easy to ignore. Now others who have the ear of the university are making similar points.

There are now much bigger names, such as Harvard philosopher Hilary Putnam, Nobel economist Amartya Sen, and Francis Fukuyama, who are forcing scholars to listen. They are pointing out the surprising fact that philosophers, scientists, and economists have never been able to absolutely separate fact and value. Facts themselves are value-laden.

As they point out, the perception or definition of facts depends on concepts, and concepts are always subject to criticism and therefore to value judgment. So perception is not just a given, if that's what where we thought facts came from. We bring some conceptual tools to our investigations, including what must be called values. Hypothesis selection in science often—maybe usually—involves values (such as coherence, simplicity, or beauty) that act like ethical values. Putnam uses the example of Einstein.

> Both Einstein's theory of gravitation and Alfred North Whitehead's 1922 theory (of which very few people have ever heard) agreed with special relativity, and both predicted the familiar phenomena of the deflection of light by gravitation, the non-Newtonian character of the orbit of Mercury, the exact orbit of the Moon, among other things. Yet Einstein's theory was accepted and Whitehead's theory was rejected fifty years before anyone thought of an observation that would decide between the two. . . . In short, judgments of coherence, simplicity, and so on are

---

2. Douglas Sloan, *Faith and Knowledge: Mainline Protestantism and American Higher Education* (Louisville: Westminster John Knox, 1994), 53–57. See also the critique of Max Weber in Leo Strauss, *Natural Right in History* (Chicago: University of Chicago Press, 1953), 35–80.

presupposed by physical science. Yet coherence, simplicity, and the like are values. Indeed, each and every one of the familiar arguments for relativism in ethics could be repeated in connection with these epistemic values.[3]

The opposite is also true, as values must be treated as facts. For Putnam goes on to show that what we call "values" are subject to the same kind of objective consideration as what we call facts. Objective value comes from the criticism of our valuations, just as science comes from criticism of observations. (Philosophy, meanwhile, is criticism of criticism.) So in principle, values can also be defended as true or attacked as false.[4] They are not simply subjective or political.

The reconsideration of a fact/value divide is bound to become part of the larger exploration of the historical origins of the concept of "fact." It is already being illuminated by scholars like Steven Shapin in his provocatively titled *A Social History of Truth*. It should be noted that such hermeneutical explorations are not meant simply to deconstruct the concept of truth, but to elaborate it.[5]

Perhaps the classic discussion remains that of British chemist Michael Polanyi, who in the 1950s detailed how science itself necessarily involves what he described as "personal knowledge." As a sample of his intricate argument:

> Only a tiny fraction of all knowable facts are of interest to scientists, and scientific passion serves also as a guide in the assessment of what is of higher and what of lesser interest; what is great in science, and what relatively slight. I want to show that this appreciation depends ultimately on a sense of intellectual beauty; that it is an emotional response which can never be dispassionately defined, any more than

3. Hilary Putnam, *The Collapse of the Fact/Value Dichotomy* (Cambridge, MA: Harvard University Press, 2002), 97, 109, 132, 142.

4. Ibid., 103, 113.

5. Steven Shapin, *A Social History of Truth: Civility and Science in Seventeenth-Century England* (Chicago: University of Chicago Press, 1994). See also Barbara Shapiro, *A Culture of Fact: England, 1550–1720* (Ithaca: Cornell University Press, 2000), and C. John Sommerville, *The News Revolution in England: Cultural Dynamics of Daily Information* (New York: Oxford University Press, 1996), 64–66.

we can dispassionately define the beauty of a work of art or the excellence of a noble action.[6]

Knowledge, proof, reality, science, even the concept of fact, are values, and part of a human reality (ontology).[7] Polanyi says this not to discredit science but to show its humanity. One hears similar things now from scientists like physicist James Cline of McGill University, who says, "I think the chances that any one of the ideas around today is true are slim. But when we do find the right answer, it will look, and smell, just right."[8]

It is relevant to my argument—that the university could profit from religious voices—that Polanyi was greatly interested in religion though not a conventional believer. It seems to have been the challenge of religious thought that raised his questions about his own scientific activities. He thought that religion's typical role was not so much to present facts as to offer a "heuristic impulse," to encourage further searching. In the midst of his technical consideration of scientific knowledge he observed that as Christianity is an exploration into facts, standards of truth and doubt are as appropriate in theological study as in science: "Theology as a whole is an intricate study of momentous problems. It is a theory of religious knowledge and a corresponding ontology of the things thus known. As such, theology reveals, or tries to reveal, the implications of religious worship, and it can be said to be true or false."

Polanyi did point out the need to preserve the boundaries appropriate to scientific and theological discourses. But he thought that they were analogous in their principles. That meant, among other things, that science could fall into absurdity in the same ways that theology might.

> Theological accounts of God must, of course, appear meaningless and often blatantly self-contradictory if taken to claim validity within the universe of observable experience. Such a result is inevitable, whenever

6. Michael Polanyi, *Personal Knowledge: Towards a Post-Critical Philosophy* (London: Routledge, 1958), 135.

7. Ibid., 380.

8. Quoted in *U.S. News and World Report* (8 September 2003), 42.

a language that is apposite to one subject matter is used with reference to another altogether different matter. The comparatively modest attempt to describe atomic processes in terms of classical electromagnetics and mechanics has led to self-contradictions which appeared no less intolerable until we eventually got accustomed to them. Today physicists enjoy these apparent absurdities which they alone can comprehend, even as [ancient theologian] Tertullian seems to have enjoyed the startling paradoxes of his faith. Far from raising doubts in my mind concerning the rationality of Christian beliefs, the paradoxes of Christianity will serve me as examples for an analogous framing and stabilizing of other beliefs by which man strives to satisfy his own self-set standards.[9]

By making an effort unusual to scientists, Polanyi was able to treat religion as the sort of thing that university scholars could turn their attention to. One would think this would be fruitful where there are ethical questions of the application of our knowledge. Thus religion might revitalize those Humanities in the Professions programs, which have a shadowy existence in the multiversity.

Our difficulty in following Polanyi's line of thought in the argument above indicates what was lost as the university simplified its notion of reality. This is not to say that we used to do better with such questions. But what Polanyi goes on to say about the contribution of vision and contemplation toward intellectual creativity suggests what we mentioned before, that time spent in the chapel might be as important as hours in the lab. For as he remarks, science, mathematics, the arts, and religion all have a role in maintaining wonder and not just explaining it.[10] Universities have too easily assumed that their job was to dispel wonder.

In the field of economics the connection of intellectual values and ethics becomes immediately obvious. Economists have felt the discomfort of the putative fact/value dichotomy especially keenly. Their subject matter, after all, is human well-being or "weal," wealth in the truest sense. That whole idea is lost when wealth is objectified in the imper-

9. Polanyi, *Personal Knowledge*, 281–282.
10. Ibid., 196–199.

sonal terms of money. Francis Fukuyama has therefore expressed an interest in showing the factual nature of economic values. The point, of course, would be to renew a dialogue between enterprise and ethics. He looks forward to a time when scholars recover the ability to argue values. It could revitalize our puzzling and inconclusive international conferences on "human rights."

Fukuyama cites Alasdair MacIntyre's observation of forty years ago, that even David Hume did not believe or practice the principle that is so often credited to him, of that gulf between fact and value.[11] And he uses several chapters in *Our Posthuman Future* to revive a concept of human nature and its corollaries. We might hope that others will engage his initiative without waiting for posthuman hybrids to force those issues.

An example of finding an *ought* in an *is* could be when we make an appeal to "human rights" or when we call for "humane" ethical action. This would mean recognizing a fact (the human difference) that not everyone accepts, and drawing conclusions that might not seem warranted. Naturalists may deny human exceptionalism and think respect for them is illogical. Yet many would think that denying that respect is naive, and that the critics' definitions of fact and reason do not stand the test of reality.

In its heyday, the fact/value dichotomy progressively narrowed the scope of the university's activities. For whenever it was discovered how values were involved with various subjects, the impulse was to drop them from explicit instruction. Values were assumed to be subjective and personal or merely traditional, and not a fruitful subject of discussion. Of course, this did not keep instructors from insinuating their values, in ways that we will consider in chapter 9.

If the new critics of the fact/value dichotomy prove successful, scholars may have to engage in more explicit debates involving values than they are trained to resolve. It will be harder to declare that such debates violate the university's essential character. It will be harder to

---

11. Francis Fukuyama, *Our Posthuman Future: Consequences of the Biotechnology Revolution* (New York: Picador, 2002), 112–115.

argue that the dichotomy justifies its secularism. So the task ahead will be to complexify things. This amounts to a reversal of the assumption, as old as the Enlightenment, that we should be striving to simplify.

The thinkers we have mentioned are of such stature that they may thus broaden the university's activities. Religion may be heard from in areas from which it was banished. For we will find that its contribution can be in perspectives and not just propositions. We have a recent model in French Protestant philosopher Jacques Ellul, who was careful not to ignore ethical aspects of his technical subjects. The old assumption has been that the university must leave it to politicians to make our choices. But there is no reason that our political debates could not begin before reaching that point. Universities might change their position in American society if they become forums for discussion of our social problems. Perhaps, given the training of the present generation of faculty, this can hardly be less than a generational change.

4

TROUBLE ELIMINATING RELIGION

I haven't yet said what I mean by "religion," while talking of the difficulties of secularism in the university. I need to do so, because we moderns have become spiritually tone-deaf and unmusical. We have fallen into the habit of seeing religion as a collection of doctrines, a thing to think about, when it can be a whole perspective or way of thinking. Readers may fear I am urging them to apply religious dogmas to our intellectual puzzles. That would rarely be possible and is hardly what I mean by accommodating religious thinking within the university.

A religious perspective could be expressed in choosing research agendas in hopes of contributing to epochal change. It could honor role models who seem possessed of transcendent insight, or seek to understand creative expressions that suggest exceptional penetration, without dissipating their insights. And in all these pursuits it would respect the intellectual virtues of hope, courage, humility, charity, thankfulness. Obviously, many academics embody these attitudes who don't think of themselves as religious, for the secularization of the university is not near to being complete. So I'm suggesting that we recognize the quasi-religious nature of what we like most about the university ideal.

Some scholars would feel comfortable entertaining the particular expressions of a religion, while others would not. This could be a welcome reminder that there is not a single orthodoxy to be promoted by the university, if only a secular one. Thus the sense that there is an idea behind or within our world could enable some to explore doctrines of creation. Concepts of incarnation might be involved in linking humanity with the image of a creator, or in understanding Jesus of Nazareth as so many have—the truth about the divine and about the human. Trinitarian theology has long been used to express the irreducible complexity of many things, including the social character of identity. The faith that overcomes nihilism and depression seems to envision something worthy of worship. We may find that such ideas extend our discussions, increase our mutual understanding, and honor our ostensible diversity.

In coming chapters we will see examples of questions that turn out to be religious in the sense that they elicit one's ultimate concerns and commitments. Admitting religious voices more frankly into university discussion might lead to joint efforts to make sense of traditional concepts that are simply dismissed today. This has never stopped happening, as historian James Turner has shown in an article tracing the origins of the West's "radical reflexivity," just-war theory, social subsidiarity, and the opening of women's history, to Christian roots.[1] For we all have the amphibious tendencies I mentioned earlier.

Things can work the other way, when religious thinkers benefit from modernity in discovering the relevance or finding new meaning in religious concepts like the personality, the image, or the grace, of God. It is strange how these have lost their resonance in societies and cultures which all depend on connections to the transcendent. Durkheim has taught us that societies die without them. But perhaps we have not entirely lost these powers of hearing.

Advocating that the university open itself to religious voices is bound to seem alarming. But this might make less difference than we think, since we maintain so many religious assumptions. As an illustration of how difficult it is to eliminate religious perspectives I'll mention another essay by historian David Hollinger. He is one of the few in the academy who has taken such matters seriously and provided thoughtful insights. As a result he was recently asked to participate in a three-year Lilly Seminar on Religion and Higher Education, in order to balance

---

1. Andrea Sterk, ed., *Religion, Scholarship, and Higher Education: Perspectives, Models, and Future Prospects* (Notre Dame: University of Notre Dame Press, 2002), 16–21.

the various religious viewpoints represented. He was an active partic-
ipant, but at the end did not think he had made his objections quite
clear. So as his contribution to the seminar's collected papers in *Religion,
Scholarship, and Higher Education: Perspectives, Models, and Future Prospects* Hollinger made one last try to show why, as he put it, "Universities
Do Not Need More Christianity."[2]

Hollinger acknowledged that religion had made vital contributions
to our intellectual heritage; and saw no reason to deny them. But the
religious voices in the seminar seemed to be asking for more. They
wanted respect shown both to the traditions and to the contemporary
expressions of the religions involved. They acted as if religion still had
something to offer and was being stifled by a hostile academic culture.

Hollinger was dubious about that and proposed a distinction to
make his objections clear. One should separate the question of the original motivation behind an contribution from the question of its current
justification. That is, we need to differentiate the origins of useful ideas
from the reasons or warrants we could now give for them. Religious
origins could be detected behind many ideas still current, but that was
of only historical interest. If they still held any importance, it was not
because of their origin but because of their current warrants. And the
proofs we use now are part of a modern epistemological system.

Religions, he says, no longer have a distinctive way of proving
things, and they don't provide our system of thought, our *episteme*.
They must adopt current epistemological standards in making their
points and must play by secular, rational rules. After all, this is what
universities are about—proving, warranting, justifying, verifying competing truth-claims. If Christianity has nothing distinctive to say along
this line, then we surely don't need more of it in the university. Maybe
we need less.

I would take issue with Hollinger here. I do not think that universities are mostly about proving things. Maybe in the sciences and engineering proof or verification are still really central, and we may think
of this as the intellectual core of the university. But in Hollinger's own
field of history, for example, his colleagues rarely argue over the warrants they use. They recognize that their readers could differ over how

2. Ibid., 40–49.

much weight to give the evidence they are able to marshal. Rather, historians argue over *interpreting* the evidence.

The goal of history as an academic discipline is more to *understand* the record than to verify elements within it. Historical method is not focused so much on compelling agreement as on reaching understanding. And it is assumed that agreement on the best understanding will probably never be universal. Interpretations are not like proofs, which are meant to compel agreement. Interpretations are offered in hopes of being convincing; they depend on the readers' understanding of human motivation in general. The humanities have long understood themselves this way, and this approach is now infiltrating the "social sciences" as well, as they also try to understand persons.

What is true of history is true of many fields. Most of the university is less interested in warrants than in interpretations or understandings. So much of the university population, after all, is in professional schools like business, education, law, journalism, public administration, fine arts, and so on. Like the humanities, these are all concerned with serving the human and must deal with values like beauty, truth, welfare, justice, happiness. They would use the notion of proof in a very loose sense, almost metaphorically. Their debates allow for some disagreement because we have different understandings of the human good and human nature. We could say that they go back to different religious views (saving this subject for chapter 5).

As a footnote, I might add that the warrants that Hollinger himself uses are related to biblical roots. His belief in the onward march of secularism is in what scholars call the "deuteronomic tradition" of a historically progressive sense, familiar from the Hebrew Bible. And the author of the Gospel According to St. Luke and the Acts of the Apostles describes his own approach as relying on evidence, rather than intuition or revelation as would be the case in other religious traditions. One can either claim that Luke was secular or acknowledge that we are part of a religious tradition.

❦

At the birth of the secular university, science quickly became the paradigm of academic activity, with its interest in proofs. This was understandable, given the decadent state of a curriculum which had grown old since the Renaissance. But the various disciplines have made such progress by now that our main problems are those of applying our new knowledge. Therefore we need to think primarily in terms of human goals and purposes. To treat humans merely as objects of positivistic study limits our considerations intolerably. We must study them hermeneutically, in terms of the things that make sense to humans, in this era of professional education.

Secular rationalism has difficulties here. The more one edges into naturalism, the harder it becomes to express human values. The university may be uneasy about using such words as "evil," "justice," "sanity," "welfare," "truth," "good," "responsibility," while the traditional personalist and religious discourses that use such terms are at least coherent. That is, we know when we have said something "ungrammatical" or absurd in such a language. We recognize when somebody is making a joke. Naturalists may assure us that someday a thoroughly naturalistic discourse will be as coherent, but they are far from offering proofs of this. It is still a matter of faith, and perhaps a waning faith at that.

In Hollinger's terms, it is not clear that we have found a secular *episteme* for our personalist terms. Our difficulty in accommodating discussions of value within the secular university indicates the opposite. But to feel that they must therefore be banished will marginalize universities further—the more so if the public sees that only certain views are banished, arbitrarily.

Even in the sciences, when we prioritize projects, it is an understanding of the human that is operating. So the applied sciences like architecture, medicine, veterinary medicine, and psychology all join the other disciplines in allowing proofs to give way to understandings.

Religious thinkers may have distinctive views on these value questions. In fact, they may have several competing views. This does not discredit the idea of religious voices in the academy any more than entertaining different philosophical, literary-critical, or historiographical voices. The social sciences argue over their competing paradigms. We could view the diversity coming from religious viewpoints as strengthening the university rather than weakening it. After all, we are not talking about forcing religious viewpoints on others. The university's openness to development was part of its medieval Christian origins, when it absorbed pagan (Greek) and Islamic contributions.

It is true that Christians need to learn to converse with secularists. They have been doing so for a long time, as Hollinger points out. Unfortunately, they may have lost the knack from being so long in the academic wilderness. But we have mentioned a resurgence in the works of religious philosophers like Ellul, MacIntyre, Hauerwas, Ricoeur, Milbank, Kolakowski, and others. What will be new is when secularists learn to acknowledge other "rationalities." The newly leveled, or scrambled, playing field could as easily be seen as a religious one as to say that Christians have adopted a secular epistemology. It should be unnecessary to decide on the one best description.

Since the Enlightenment, certain elements have been fighting against the religious language we inherited for discussion of human life. This is understandable, given the restrictions that churches once put on inquiry and the sins they committed in an era of religious compulsion. But instead of competing for hegemony we could go forward to an era of real diversity, in which religious viewpoints would be entertained and explored rather than dismissed. It was doubtless necessary to see how far we could deconstruct or "reduce" the terms we inherited to lower conceptual levels. But when we see them still standing, the time has come to resume their exploration. For nobody is arguing that ethics and other human concerns are becoming less important just because we are finding it harder to discuss them.

Many think that religion is the enemy of diversity and tolerance. This even serves ironically as the justification for not tolerating it. But we have the word of Stanley Fish himself, who helped put postmodernism on the map, that this can go too far.

Fish was reacting to a criticism of Christian fundamentalists by two prominent "liberal" political philosophers, and he faulted the latter for their own lack of tolerance. In connection with a ruling on religion in the public schools, Amy Gutmann and Dennis Thompson had criticized those presenting religious "arguments" for only pretending to appeal to shared or disinterested principle. They held that any dogmatic arguments would fall short of the moral argumentation appropriate to political debate. But Fish thinks that the same could be said of Gutmann and Thompson's position. He thinks he sees the same amount of principle in the religious viewpoints, and perhaps less self-deception.

Fish calls Gutmann and Thompson's arguments "dismissive gestures" that only pretend to answer their opponents while ensuring the outcomes fashionable among their academic friends. In short, they showed the same closed-mindedness they accuse religious persons of having. While pretending to embody general rules, which they announce as "disinterested" and "impartial," their principles primarily serve to exclude opposing views in advance.

Fish claims that their treatment of the famous *Mozert* case, concerning objectionable textbooks, illustrates this.

> The argument of the fundamentalist parents, they say, "ignored a simple distinction between teaching students about a religion and teaching them to believe in a religion." But what they . . . fail to understand is that the distinction between "teaching about" and "teaching to believe in"—between exposure and indoctrination—rests on a psychology that is part and parcel of the liberalism Vicki Frost and her friends don't want imposed on their children. In that [secularist] psychology, the mind remains unaffected by the ideas and doctrines that pass before it, and its job is to weigh and assess those doctrines from a position distanced from and independent of any one of them. (Note how this picture of the mind is a microcosm of the liberal society in which it operates and flourishes.) . . .
>
> In this [religious] psychology (of which there are secular analogues), exposure is not an innocent or healthy experience, but one fraught with dangers. The chief danger is not any particular doctrine to which the children might be exposed but the unannounced yet powerfully assumed doctrine of exposure as a first principle, as a virtual theology. . . . What the children are being indoctrinated in is distrust of any belief that has not been arrived at by the exercise of their unaided reason as it surveys all the alternatives before choosing one freely with no guidance from any external authority . . . and moreover, that the ideology of preferring no point of view to another is neutral.

Defendant Vicki Frost's reliance on authority could, Fish thinks, be considered an exercise of principle and justified on historical or other grounds. The secular liberal perspective at issue, by contrast, is essentially the refusal of any commitment to principle.

> It is not accurate to characterize these [liberal] men and women as "morally committed," for what they are committed to is not their morality but the deliberative process to which their morality is delivered up on the way, perhaps, to being abandoned. What they are committed to is the deferring of commitment in favor of an ever-attenuated "conversation" whose maintenance is the only value they wholeheartedly embrace.[3]

The fact that Fish could intelligently entertain the ideas of fundamentalists while not accepting them personally casts doubt on the argument that those religious ideas are "inaccessible" in public debate. Likewise, the fact that it took a secularist like Fish to explain the basis of the religious position should earn the appreciation of the religious, who may need that perspective to help understand themselves. It is not impossible to enter dialogue with religious views, so long as one's mind is open to the possibility that they may have some substance. Universities today, however, are in a mood to censor the views in advance, justified by laws that forbid us from imposing religious views—a point dealt with in chapter 7. Fish may even be acknowledging that the fundamentalists' point occurred to them precisely because of their position outside the mainstream. That is a point I would stress in general to those who see that the academy is an increasingly sterile environment.

It will be hard for religion to shake our assumption that it has always been the block to tolerance. This assumption can be seen in the condemnation of any form of proselytizing for one's beliefs. Ironically, this hyperliberal emphasis itself amounts to proselytizing for tolerance! Understood properly, toleration means allowing for proselytizing, not stifling it. For proselytizing implies the freedom of one's audience, as op-

---

3. Stanley Fish, "Mutual Respect as a Device of Exclusion," in *Deliberative Politics: Essays on Democracy and Disagreement*, ed. Stephen Macedo (New York: Oxford University Press, 1999), 92–95. Gutmann and Thompson sought to answer Fish's argument (257–259).

posed to efforts to coerce it. Stifling religious views may show a lack of confidence.

Secularists were not always thus. In 1867, just before the push toward secular universities began, the prominent liberal philosopher John Stuart Mill was named to the honorary position of Rector of St. Andrews University in Scotland. His inaugural address described what he thought should guide university reform, and unfortunately it sounds too much like a treatise on logic, his special subject. But he was also insistent that "It is a very imperfect education which trains the intelligence only, but not the will. . . . The moral or religious influence which a university can exercise, consists less in any express teaching, than in the pervading tone of the place. . . . It should present all knowledge as chiefly a means to worthiness of life." Mill thought that this would largely be done informally, through personal influence: "There is nothing which spreads more contagiously from teacher to pupil than elevation of sentiment."[4]

It is interesting that this thoroughgoing secularist should still think that religion of some kind would characterize any education worthy of the name. Of course, he felt that it should have to compete with the other "principal systems of moral philosophy, . . . the Aristotelian, the Epicurean, the Stoic, the Judaic, the Christian in the various modes of its interpretation. . . . [But] I do not mean that [the curriculum] should encourage an essentially sceptical eclecticism." His regret at that time was that "the great question of the relation of education to religion" was suffering from the dogmatism of the religious on one hand and secularists on the other.[5]

What Mill might sense today is a triumph of secular dogmatism. Postmodernists have renewed Mill's attack on the most confining features of "the Enlightenment project," without being any more welcoming to religious viewpoints.

4. John Stuart Mill, "Inaugural Address at St. Andrews," in *The Six Great Humanistic Essays of John Stuart Mill* (New York: Washington Square, 1963), 350.
5. Ibid., 351–352.

We can't seem to transcend a personalist vocabulary, whatever its warrants turn out to be. It appears that one must choose the approach appropriate to the subject matter at hand, and when we probe our ideas with regard to the human we find our beliefs at the bottom. Of course, universities exist in order to probe beneath prejudice. But we don't find that the sciences are inexorably yielding to physicalist reductions. The humanities are finding it awkward to deconstruct their defining term. So we might think of acknowledging the existing standoff, instead of feeling that we must press on with some secular or antireligious understanding of the subject.

Think of the corollaries of the human. While some instances of "justice" can be seen to be unjust, this doesn't dissolve the idea of justice; it makes the contrast all the more striking. Freud might tell us what we are most likely to feel guilty about, but that does not dispense with the abstract concept of guilt. On the other hand, one can hardly imagine a religion that did not involve the whole range of personalist terms and integrate them into larger themes like creation, fall, redemption, and judgment. From here, they may open into other areas like our political thinking, where neuroscience or physics are no help.

We have already spoken of the new recognition of narrative, and how it recognizes the primary reality of the personal. The linguistic turn in philosophy also suggested that language and human consciousness is constitutive of our reality. So the time may not be far off when a religious discourse is admitted as an acceptable idiom, for the aid of its suppressed and nearly forgotten intellectual heritage. This might, however, go counter to the university's traditional expectation of finding a single discourse that would mediate all thinking.

Steven Shapin's fascinating *A Social History of Truth* alerts us to one more way that religion continues to underpin our universities. Shapin, a historian of science, was struck by how difficult it was to get modern science up and running, given the huge suspicions there were of the printed word in seventeenth-century Europe. Historians of printing had earlier pointed out that the invention of printing did not automatically increase knowledge. It often increased nonsense, spreading fictions as truth, mass-producing error and initially giving more of a boost to astrology than to science. To establish serious standards of scholarly truth in publishing, trust had to be established among writers. This took some effort, which Shapin describes. The virtue that underlay this effort was honor, the code of a gentleman.[6]

Honor depends on pride and class prejudice, being the focal point of a self-regarding value system. Scientists had to invest honor with an importance that makes strange reading today. It served its purpose in guaranteeing and enforcing scholarly standards when they were new and unfamiliar. But of course the aristocratic class character of the enterprise would have to find a replacement, as more religious and democratic standards prevailed in Victorian times. One might suppose that utilitarian values would do as well. But we may doubt this when we read reports that currently "one-third of scientists surveyed said that within the previous three years, they had engaged in at least one [professional] practice that would probably get them into trouble."[7] What restrained the other two-thirds? One might guess that it was some vestige of a religious code.

Honor is an older code than what we like to call the "Protestant ethic," and it has not worn as well. Universities continue to depend on its religious replacements, as do so many other institutions today. University teaching and advising, as well as scholarship and publishing, obviously depend on something more than capitalist or sociobiological self-interest.

A final point about the effort to eliminate religion from academic life may seem an odd one. It concerns the very common claim of having lost one's religious faith sometime in childhood. Failure to have done so would be a matter for worry among academics. They express dismay at students who did not follow suit.

When one loses one's religion at that age, of course, religion will always thereafter seem childish. If one were encouraged to explore and

6. Steven Shapin, *A Social History of Truth: Civility and Science in Seventeenth-Century England* (Chicago: University of Chicago Press, 1994).
7. *Gainesville Sun* (9 June 2005), report taken from *Nature*.

develop religious observance and considerations into adulthood, they would have a chance to deepen. If the baby had been saved while the bathwater was being tossed, it might have grown up. University culture doesn't encourage that, or even acknowledge the notion of a mature faith.

It might seem a stretch to blame this pattern on university secularization. But try to imagine a scenario in which the public knew that universities were respectful of religious thinkers. It might then be familiar with the names of theologians like Niebuhr, Tillich, Tracy, and Urs von Balthasar, and perhaps even with ideas they were associated with. Churches themselves would take the intellectual dimension of their faith more seriously. Even Sunday school teachers might engage young people with something of more substance. American society might have more intellectual substance, if children did not have to wait so long to be challenged to think.

What seems to happen instead is that parents as well as teachers absorb the idea that religion has no intellectual dimension. Journalists are not challenged to develop a more sophisticated paradigm of religion. This may be one area of American life in which university intellectuals are offering leadership, in convincing us that religion has no intellectual dimension.

When Neil Postman was lamenting "the end of education," he pointed out that "without a purpose, schools are houses of detention." While religion should offer a sense of purpose, he feared that even the study of comparative religion was largely for purposes of "narrative busting." Being Jewish, Postman was naturally concerned that public schools not favor one religion over others. But still he argued, "It is quite impossible for anyone to claim to be educated who has no knowledge of the role played by religion in the formation of culture."[8] This would not actually amount to religious education, but even this would require the adoption of some intellectual virtues that we find in short supply these days: respect, appreciation, genuine tolerance.

The marginalization of religion, promoted by officially secular universities and seeping downward, conceals the ways in which those same

---

8. Neil Postman, *The End of Education: Redefining the Value of School* (New York: Alfred A. Knopf, 1995), 7, 151–154.

universities depend on religious concepts and concerns. Our persisting sense of the intellectual and social virtues that underpin honest scholarship and instruction suggests the need for nurturing what have been thought of as religious attitudes. The life of the university, as well as its product, shows vestiges of its religious origins.

Somehow the American public has managed to resist the secularist thrust of the university. But there has been damage to the intellectual life of the nation, to say nothing of the patriotism associated with our "civil religion." In 1940 Americans had to answer the question of whether democracy was worth dying for, after having heard it roundly criticized by university intellectuals during the trying times of the depression.[9] At a time when human life itself is becoming a political and social issue, we may face something like that uncertainty as we move into the future.

9. Edward A. Purcell Jr., *The Crisis of Democratic Theory: Scientific Naturalism and the Problem of Value* (Lexington: University Press of Kentucky, 1973), 156.

5

TROUBLE JUDGING RELIGIONS

The end of the Cold War has made us more aware of the religious divisions of the world that are continuing strongly into our third millennium. There is good reason for thinking that much of the world's conflict is religious, although academics strenuously protested Samuel Huntington's effort to point this out.[1] In fact, academics seem oddly nervous in hearing judgments on religion. Many who are happy to criticize religion in general are averse to hearing any one religion singled out. Universities cannot afford such timidity if they are to offer leadership in debating real-world issues. Academics long neglected the study of religions, thinking that they were headed for extinction in the process of modernization. So it may seem odd now to think that reasoned judgment on them is a responsibility of the university.

It is not as though secular academics don't have feelings on this subject. But they don't have an active vocabulary with which to discuss it. They know that the general public—including legislators, taxpayers, parents, students—has a vague feeling that religion is a good thing, and perhaps even the embodiment of the good. So there is a question of how scholars can register disapproval without seeming merely dismis-

---

1. Samuel P. Huntington, *The Clash of Civilizations and the Remaking of World Order* (New York: Simon and Schuster, 1996). See some of his critics in *Foreign Affairs* 72:4 (September/October 1993): 2–26.

sive. In short, they need to consider how to judge religion or religions and by what standards.

We are tempted to want to talk about religion in general, in its relation to politics, society, or thought. But with the increasing contention between religions it is becoming clear that there is no such thing as religion-in-general. There are specific religions, and they differ dramatically. They have changed over time, and there are even important divisions within them. Religion per se is only an analytical term, referring to a certain kind of response to a certain kind of power.[2] But in proceeding into this area we will need to know which religion or which understanding of religion we are talking about.

Judging religions may involve more than considering whole religious systems, using their official statements. We may also want to judge individual adherents. They may fall short of what we think is the best understanding of their own tradition, or might actually improve on it, from our point of view. We probably will not be persuaded by their own judgments in such matters, being unable to ignore our own standards. But to profess no judgment at all is to treat them as members of another species.

The destruction of the World Trade Center has focused attention on the issue, and also on our awkwardness in expressing ourselves. Muslims attacked Christians and Jews, because they were Christians and Jews, and rejoiced at their success. Some of them said they were responding to the Crusades, which astonished us, who are also critical of crusading if we remember it at all. The initial reaction of secularist academics was often to minimize the religious element involved. Scholars and journalists joined in denying that the attack of 9/11 should be seen as religious. News articles declared that this is not really what Islam teaches and parsed quotations from the Qur'an that sound more peaceable.

No doubt they were afraid that someone might feel religiously su-

---

2. That is, religion cannot be given a substantive, referential, or real definition, as all writers on the subject agree. For this nominal and analytical definition, see C. John Sommerville, "Resurrecting Religion in a New (Hermeneutical) Dimension," *Fides et Historia* 30 (1998): 21–30, which argues that only a nominal definition (of the word), rather than a "real" definition (of the thing), will work with regard to "religion," given the disputes concerning matters of reference. For more, see further in this chapter.

perior. Journalists and academics have for some time been promoting a doctrine of moral equivalency, which amounts to the idea that there's not that much difference between cultures. At least there is too much blame to spread around for anyone to be passing moral judgment. Above all, that judgment should not come from rival religions.

But if this is going to be the shape of the world in our lifetimes, keeping a silence on the subject emphasizes the irrelevance of the secular university. We should also note that our domestic political parties are showing a contrasting religious coloration. We have an increasingly hard time being polite about the public effects of religion. Which means that we cannot have reasoned discussions, as we might if there were some academic leadership on the subject.

The secular university's long lack of interest in religion now shows. Students will tell you that the slightest mention of religion in their classes will be the occasion for some dismissive gesture or sly ridicule. But the loss of knowledge about religions has not made us more sophisticated in dealing with the subject. We have been conditioned (rather than taught) to ignore or deny differences and to dismiss religions equally. This may be meant as a kindness. Academics are guilty of an "essentialism" that sees religion as something one has no control over, like a birthmark that we all try to ignore. Persons who are themselves religious naturally find it easier to make distinctions, but they will not be leading the discussion.

The most unsettling aspect of all this is that a religion can be judged only on the basis of another religion. When you are through formulating your criteria and your judgment, you will notice that they amount to your own religious stance. You may not have realized you had such a thing, but it will have all the earmarks of what theologian Paul Tillich called your "ultimate concern."

One could try to dismiss all religion (generically) as an illusion. There have been numerous efforts to explain what is behind it all. There are none, however, that the sociologists, anthropologists, and psychologists involved would all agree on. Partly this is because scholars accept the view that religion cannot be defined, and they have very different things in mind when they try to explain it. They are explaining away different things. There is obviously a difference between showing that a particular religious practice or belief betrays some mundane origin, and showing that they all do. One reaction to these difficulties is to hold that what they consider pathological strains are not religion at all and call them something like "fundamentalism," "superstition," or "fanaticism." Or one could allow that there must be something real at its basis, but that particular expressions of it are bound to be deficient. Rejecting religion-in-general proves an elusive task.

When it comes to particular religions, our reaction is to look for some nonreligious basis from which to judge them—some scientific or ethical basis, for instance. Religions are often contrasted with science as an intellectual method, to show that they are not good science. But religions rarely claim to be science, in our sense of the word. Ethical judgments come from particular ethical perspectives, and at most, it would only be the ethics of the religion that would be faulted. Similarly, appealing to a "perennial philosophy" would show only that the religion was deficient as a philosophy. But again, religions claim to be more than what we nominally define as philosophy.

So we commonly make rather offhand judgments of what is "good" (healthy, true, reasonable) in the area of religion. William James propounded a pragmatic test, which begged all the questions. Judge them by their fruits, he said.[3] That came directly from the Sermon on the Mount, as he knew, indicating the difficulty of finding a basis outside religion. Some may think that rationalism is based in self-validating principles, or that "simple logic" would settle these matters. Nel Nodding's recent book bears the title Educating for Intelligent Belief or Unbelief.[4] That sounds promising, but it gets things backward.

Belief is not built on intelligence. Rather, intelligence is built on belief. We're talking about the intelligence of philosophers as well as of everyone else. Belief amounts to the assumptions, the prereflective commitments, that lie beneath our thinking. What we call logic works on the basis of beliefs to produce ideas. So logic does not mean the amount

3. William James, The Varieties of Religious Experience (London: Longmans, Green, 1908), 20–21.

4. Nel Noddings, Educating for Intelligent Belief or Unbelief (New York: Teachers College Press, 1993).

of truth in our thinking, but the amount of consistency in it. All intellectual systems go down to such assumptions or beliefs. Beliefs can be proven or disproven only within a system of beliefs, not singly, even in science. One finds these ideas developed in Elmer John Thiessen's *Teaching for Commitment*.[5]

Alasdair MacIntyre has emphasized this ultimacy of beliefs in works like *Whose Justice? Which Rationality?* (1988) and *Three Rival Versions of Moral Enquiry* (1990). In them, he stressed that there is not just one thing we call rationality. There are different "traditions" of rationality, and he describes the liberal, Aristotelian, Augustinian, Scottish Common-Sense versions, and others. He provocatively terms these "traditions"—a word that was always used to mean "mindless," to make his point. They are, he says, different intellectual cultures, any one of which is coherent enough to sustain wide intellectual debate, but all of which argue from different assumptions. Rationality means consistency or coherence *within* one or another of these traditions. At least some of these traditions of rationality may be viewed as religious, which he thinks is no disqualification.

We have long since absorbed the fact that science itself, our model for all of knowledge, is not simply self-evidently true. Western science did not discover nature's regularity, but began by assuming it. If scientists had not assumed regularity, they would never have worked to find its detailed character. And it is almost an axiom of the history of science that Western science originated in a monotheistic metaphysics, which explains why other civilizations have been working on different lines. Another assumption of our science is that one can get true knowledge from studying only part of the whole. That is, we can find the "laws" of a part of a universe, while assuming the world to be pluralistic. So we have not an inductive science, in which details are derived logically from first principles, but an empirical one, whose basis sometimes shifts.

Of late, we have become more aware of how these intellectual cultures have a tendency to reflect particular social conditions, so that liberal rationalism can be associated with bureaucratic economic and

5. Elmer John Thiessen, *Teaching for Commitment* (Montreal: McGill-Queen's University Press, 1993), 70, 111, drawing on W. V. Quine and others.

political institutions and the individualism they foster. It may rightly be preferred for that reason. But it would be naive to claim that it was therefore uniquely "based on logic and reason."

We are apt to think that the assumptions underlying a religion, like Christianity, will be much stranger than the assumptions of science. But that is not necessarily true. One possible religious assumption (perhaps not universal) is that there is a bright line between the human and the rest of nature. Secularist naturalism has an issue with this, holding that everything is derived from the same stuff. But as we saw in chapter 2, it is not the religious assumption that turns out to be bizarre. It is naturalism that strains belief and that we constantly ignore, revealing an unshakeable intuition of the human difference. The upshot is that most everyone holds beliefs related to both evolution and creation, to anticipate our next chapter.

So the assumptions of our sciences are appropriate to an enterprise with limited aims. Taking it as the model for all academic judgment limits the university's scope. The university's logic can tell us is whether one's religious statements are self-consistent, but not whether they are true. That is what the author of *Educating for Intelligent Belief or Unbelief* had in mind. But questions of ultimate truth would get us into the area of religion, where we feel a little out of place. Our question is whether the university could at least host discussions involving MacIntyre's particular religious traditions. Can we really engage the diversity that we think has such creative potential? Or must such discussions seek another venue?

The point, so far, is that whatever basis we find for judging religion turns out to be our religion. It represents whatever we give our ultimate devotion to. So we should not assume, too quickly, that there is some "secular" perspective. We will need to come back, however, to the problem of defining religion.

One might think that the religious studies departments at secular universities were established precisely for the purpose of applying rational criteria to a consideration of religions. Are they given to exercising judgment in this area?

Departments of Religion on secular campuses are in a sensitive position with respect to this question. They have adopted the objectivity held up as the universal standard of rationality, meaning that they often prefer to view religion from the outside rather than the inside. They feel they must strive to be fair to all traditions, hold them all at a distance, and not appear to be preaching. So religions tend to be treated as equally important or interesting, which seems to suggest the importance of religion but the unimportance of any particular religion.

It is rather like learning Language without learning any particular language. For as we move beyond a bare religious awareness, religions are radically different. Students of "comparative religion" constantly warn against the assumption that all religions teach the same thing.[6] Among the notable early efforts in sociology were Max Weber's investigations into how the massive differences between the world's civilizations centered in their religions. But even those scholars, in their efforts to create a comparative science of religion, sometimes forget just how incommensurable religions can be.

In different studies, Professors J. A. DiNoia and S. Mark Heim tried to emphasize the futility of finding a single thing called "religion." They explored the extent to which different religions have not only different beliefs but radically different goals. They complain that among students of religion, true relativists are rare. Most teach either that religions are different paths to the same goal (pluralism) or that they are essentially the same path (inclusivism). Scholars are tempted to assert a core philosophy contained in them all, perhaps to save the reputation of religion among their secularist colleagues, showing that no religion can be wrong if understood properly. But Heim parodies this denial of meaningful difference with his fable of the "Idea of Travel."

> It is as if we were faced with a number of different tickets (train, boat, plane, bus), each with distinctive maps and itineraries attached. Those who favor a pluralist theory . . . could maintain that because travel of any sort involves some constant generic elements (tickets have a price; some representation of the path is needed; we will never depart if we don't show up on time) it is false and arrogant to suppose that we would miss something on one trip we might find on another or that we don't

---

6. E.g., Jonathan Z. Smith, *Imagining Religion: From Babylon to Jonestown* (Chicago: University of Chicago Press, 1982), 102–120.

all have the same destination. There is, after all, only one world. And these trips are all ways of relating to it. . . .

It would be relentlessly (and rightly) insisted that none of the maps or itineraries provides a "literal" representation of its destination or of the trip itself. Instead we will be told it is "traveling" as a human condition, "arrival" as the subjective realization of a sense of completion, and "the Destination" as the ultimate ground of the possibility of any arrival which are truly real. Jaffna, Kyoto, Santiago de Compostela are mythical forms of "The Destination."[7]

DiNoia wryly recounts the tale of the Buddhist scholar who studied the lives of Catholic saints, sadly concluding that they were bad Buddhists.[8]

Religious studies departments come closest to expressing their judgment when they treat the religious heritage of their majority students with condescension. The irony is that this self-deprecation is actually an expression of a Christian virtue, of humility and repentance. We discover the ways that attitudes like these have made us unique only by visiting other cultures.

Nevertheless, it is right for them to want to express judgment. No intelligent person can avoid doing so; it is what we mean by intelligence. The pretense to indifference is transparent. The familiar complaints about Christianity involve the Crusades, the Inquisition, the religious wars of 1550–1650, persecution of witches, slavery, racism, oppression of women, anti-Semitism, opposition to science. In nineteenth-century America these were initially raised by Protestants seeking to discredit the Catholic church and especially its feared parochial educational efforts. Surely it was one of our public schools' most successful educational efforts. But we need to recognize the obvious basis for such judgments.

A Socratic education would ask what one's general reaction is to that list of Christianity's sins. Why are we agreed that they are deplorable? Who taught us to recognize them as evil? For a start, they all violate a religion of love. Not all religions elevate love to a first principle, and none may be entirely consistent. But Christianity eventually judged

---

7. S. Mark Heim, *Salvations: Truth and Difference in Religion* (Maryknoll, NY: Orbis, 1995), 219–220.

8. J. A. DiNoia, *The Diversity of Religions* (Washington: Catholic University Press, 1992), 34.

them to be abuses. Having been raised in a culture with a Christian scaling of values, there is no need to look further for the source of our revulsion. The criticisms were religious in their origin.

One might think there would be some enlightened, utilitarian standard that they violate, some drastic imbalance between pain and pleasure. But one could never weigh the pleasure and pain from such events for a single individual, let alone for a whole society, and for all future generations. Surely it is the horror and the injustice of the events that we have in mind, whether we profess Christianity or not. And the feeling that Christians should have known better.

Other religions might make very different judgments. Crusades may have been an aberration for Christians, but not for others. We might imagine that ethics are somehow self-evident and that calling our standards "Christian" is a bit provincial. But in fact, ethics are highly relative. That is, they are "related" to particular ways of life. And religions are like Wittgenstein's different "ways of life," with their different language-games.

To show how widely ethical standards can differ, I offer my students the following example. When the Anglo-Saxons in England adopted Christianity, they may not have entirely understood what they were buying into. The values their leaders had always found self-evident were the values associated with the concept of honor, which means earning and insisting on respect from others. By contrast, the values self-evident to the Christian missioners were the values of charity, meaning wanting the best for others.

To see the difference, I ask students to imagine seeing someone coming down the street toward them at night, with a big purse under her arm. It occurs to you that there might be something you wanted in that purse and that you could knock her over and take it. But you don't. Why not? You might think that there could be someone watching, and that you could get into trouble for doing that. At the least, people might despise you for being the sort of person who picked on the weak. In other words, you would be thinking entirely of yourself, of your honor or reputation, not of the little old lady.

But your train of thought could have been quite different. You might have put yourself in her shoes and thought how unpleasant being mugged would be. Others might be depending on her, and the suffering you cause would spread even further. In short, you are taking others into consideration and wanting the best for them.

An ethical system based in honor is a self-regarding ethic, while one based in charity is an other-regarding ethic. My point is that they are equally self-evident to those who grow up with them. But think of their corollaries. With honor goes a concentration on pride rather than humility, dominance rather than service, courage rather than peaceableness, glory rather than modesty, loyalty rather than respect for all, generosity to one's friends rather than equality. Charity expresses the contrasting values in each of these pairs. Students only have to see this comparison on the blackboard to realize how Christian their moral orientation still is. Today, the ethic of honor describes the values of a street gang. Better than nothing, maybe, but we wouldn't want to move to that neighborhood.

The Anglo-Saxons took a long time absorbing the values preached by the monks. They couldn't see how any society could survive that did not respect strength. They twisted Christianity into something that could preach the Crusades, which were to protect God's honor. A medieval division of labor left women and serfs and monks to specialize in the charitable virtues.

The point is that we can criticize Christian practice on the basis of specifically Christian values. In effect, we will be asking for more of it, or a purer strain. To give up Christian standards would leave us with no basis for our criticisms. Nobody since Nietzsche has criticized Christians for being too peaceable, too charitable.

In short, we judge other religions on the basis of our own religion. Indeed, we discover what our actual religion is by the judgments we render. This does not mean, however, that prophetic (alien) voices might not sometimes break through and challenge us. Those can be exciting, uncomfortable times. But again, our religious heritage itself encourages us to live under judgment.

Our most important judgments will transcend utilitarianism and brush against religious commitments. But even the smaller ones may well do so. Take, for example, the questions of whether it is better to prolong all human lives whatever the cost or to redirect resources to free up hospital beds for some other purpose. We won't be satisfied to argue that simply in terms of dollars. It is natural to argue in terms of ethical views involving notions of the human. This might be done within a single religion or between religions, while science will contribute technical details to the debate. Should insane persons be executed for their crimes? Should anybody be executed for their crimes? Is the whole idea of crime too relative to take seriously? To imagine that we could conclude such debates without involving our ultimate views is unrealistic. We should not be afraid to recognize that we are arguing from something like a religious base, as if there was an alternative.

Once we have such arguments, we will find that religions differ radically. Does this mean that such disagreements can never be resolved? It may mean that. But the goal of discussion might not be agreement, but rather understanding. We might still learn to respect those who disagree radically. Practice at judging should make us all more conscious that our own basic orientations are not self-evident.

Facing up to the religious basis of our judgments may bring about religious conversions or deconversions. We may convince others of the "truths" of our faith, or find our own faith shifting. Proselytizing is viewed with horror by academics as an intolerable assault on personal identity. The same horror may be missing when professors assault students' birthright beliefs. But we could avoid this awkwardness if views were exchanged with due respect for the strengths of the various positions. Even "relativism" is justified when one actually shows what something is related to, rather than invoked as a skeptical cliché.

Finally, we must say something about the secular university's notorious inability even to define religion. For it is a notable example of the difficulties that secularism has gotten itself into. Given the number of Departments of Religious Studies, it is a serious matter that they cannot define their field. Their reluctance to do so is related to intellectual commitments they made at the outset of the secularist experiment.

Religious scholars will object that there is no possibility of defining a subject, religion, that is so diverse as to exhibit no really universal features. This sounds straightforward but actually contains an error: the notion that all definitions should be referential or "real" definitions. They assume that definitions work by referring a word to a thing. But there is another type of definition called a "nominal" definition. It compares a word to other words, or shows the way it is used in discourse. So it is the difference between defining a thing and defining a word. The approach one takes is determined by the "thing" to be defined.

Religion, of all things, is least likely to be susceptible to a referential definition, because its supposed object is so elusive. That elusiveness—religions' ineffable aspects—is almost a defining characteristic, after all. So in defining "religion" we should recognize that we are defining a word and not a thing. In an article on the subject, I concluded that the way English-speakers use the word suggests that religion is a word we use for (in brief) a certain kind of response to a certain kind of power. The response and the power are understood to be unique, beyond anything else in our experience.[9]

My experience in trying to promote this understanding shows that scholars are insistent in their objection to it. They seem determined to objectify their subject. That is the way of modern scholarship. They would like to create a science of comparative religion, and for that they need to have handles on the object of study. After all, viewing religion from the inside is what theologians do, and secular universities would not hire theologians. (Cultural studies scholars also view religions from the inside, but only to change it into something else, and not to treat it in its own terms.)

You might object that scholars are also beginning from linguistic usage, since English-speakers do call all these things religions, like Buddhism, Voodoo, and Gnosticism. So even going by language, shouldn't we be trying to find universal features among agreed examples? The problem is that it was not until the nineteenth-century that English-speakers (missionaries and early sociologists) dubbed these things "religions." To this day, Asian scholars complain that the English word doesn't really apply to their cultures, and American textbooks always mention in passing that there are problems in applying the word to certain forms of, say, Buddhism. So they are admitting that social use hasn't really changed the word to suit the scholars. But they don't draw the obvious conclusion: that some societies may not have religions in our sense of the term. We think that would be insulting to those groups,

9. See note 2 above.

or that we would be revealing the provincial nature of our culture and language.

But all languages are provincial. Only scientific discourse and mathematics transcend linguistic boundaries. "Religion" is used differently in English than in French, and the effort to create a scientific, universal language in this area is doomed. The English word has proven very durable, resisting academic efforts to shape it to their purposes. It evolved to fit our Jewish and Christian heritage, which explains why so many feel the need to coin a new term, "spirituality," for the more diverse situation today. This is wiser than the effort to impose the word "religion" imperialistically on cultures that don't recognize themselves in it. And it is symbolic of the way in which religions must be listened to in rendering our intellectual and moral judgments.

In the last sixty years, American jurisprudence has been beset with the problem of submitting religion to judgment. The efforts to be respectful have been worthy of a democracy, but the results have been uncertain. Law review articles may advise judges to consult with scholars in religious studies to help them define the term when they encounter problems in this area.[10] But this is a case where the secular university may be little help. Scholars are insistent on the differences between religions but are less clear on the ways that we must judge them. There is no avoiding such judgment, as religions are proving their resilience. And the notion that all such judgments will reveal one's own religion, however submerged and unacknowledged, may prove especially unwelcome.

10. Winnifred Fallers Sullivan, "Judging Religion," *Marquette Law Review* 81 (1998): 441–460.

6

SCIENCE GETS STRANGE

A century ago science expressed confidence that it was banishing mystery and pushing the frontiers of knowledge outward in every direction. Various academic fields wanted to be thought of as sciences, to gain respect. Science is now taken for granted, to be sure, but we seem to have gained a greater recognition of its limits. It will not answer our most pressing personal questions, cannot set its own agenda, and has no practical goals of its own. What is more surprising is the willingness of some scientists these days to use a religious language to express their sense of the mystery that they find at its frontiers.

I am not speaking here of the current arguments over "intelligent design." Some may imagine that such theories amount to something like a religious explanation, but this indicates a confusion. If science were to establish the "reality" of religion within scientific or natural terms, it would thereby cease to be religion and would become science. In English usage, "science" is our term for those aspects of reality which we can bring under our explanatory models, while "religion" is our term for that which transcends the ordinary, and for its demands on us.[1] By definition in Western languages, the natural and the religious are contrasted, though they may share "reality" between them. So as open-minded a scientist as physicist Paul Davies observes that "proof"

1. Again, see C. John Sommerville, "Resurrecting Religion in a New (Hermeneutical) Dimension," *Fides et Historia* 30 (1998): 20–31.

of intelligent design would make the origin of life not so much religious as "utterly mysterious."[2]

What I am referring to is something different, but equally mysterious. It is more in line with the scientists' mystical sense of the "non-triviality of reality."[3] As Wittgenstein put this point, science is about *how* the world is, while mysticism is the uncanny awareness *that* the world is. In his own words, "Not *how* the world is, is the mystical, but *that* it is."[4]

It is a commonplace among historians that modern science was nurtured by the monotheistic metaphysics of Western religions. Albert Einstein was famous for claiming even more: that not only the cognitive basis but also the affective or emotional drive behind science must be religious.

> Cosmic religious feeling is the strongest and noblest incitement to scientific research. . . . What a deep conviction of the rationality of the universe . . . Kepler and Newton must have had to enable them to spend years of solitary labour in disentangling the principles of celestial mechanics! Those whose acquaintance with scientific research is derived chiefly from its practical results easily develop a completely false notion of the mentality of the men who, surrounded by a sceptical world, have shown the way. . . . It is cosmic religious feeling that gives a man strength of this sort. A contemporary has said, not unjustly, that in this materialistic age of ours the serious scientific workers are the only profoundly religious people.[5]

If he was right, not only religious thinking but even a religious *awareness* may undergird scientific discovery.

Many leading scientists are becoming comfortable with such language, leaving their secularity in a sort of suspension, at least in their popular writings. Of course, religions expect to admit some mystery

2. Paul Davies, *The Fifth Miracle: The Search for the Origin and Meaning of Life* (New York: Simon and Schuster, 1999), 31.

3. Willem B. Drees, *Religion, Science and Naturalism* (Cambridge: Cambridge University Press, 1996), 114–115.

4. Ludwig Wittgenstein, *Tractatus Logico-Philosophicus* (1922; reprint, New York: Routledge, 1990), 187.

5. Albert Einstein, *The World As I See It* (London: John Lane, The Bodley Head, 1941), 27–28.

beyond their statements. But the same can be said of some sciences now, notably at the extremes of quantum physics and cosmology, the tiny and the huge. We are warned that even though the statistical expressions of quantum physics work for practical purposes, we cannot get beyond them to anything we could visualize. And as physicist John Wheeler admits, "Until we see the quantum principle with this simplicity we can well believe that we do not know the first thing about the universe, about ourselves, and about our place in the universe."[6] One could almost say that quantum physics is "an explanation of what we don't understand," to use an oxymoron once reserved for a suspect religion.

Cambridge physicist and theologian John Polkinghorne makes a similar point, observing that the Enlightenment's "clockwork universe could not survive the dissolution of the picturable and predictable into the cloudy and fitful" world of quantum theory. Nor is a recognition of nature's unpredictability found only at the micro scale of quantum events. It is also apparent at the macro level of chaotic systems, indicating an "openness" at the level of the human lifeworld.[7] Thus there is now wonder and mystery on the boundaries of science that suggests a religious awareness if not a religious response.

Physics has always inspired reflections on what is taken to be basic or ultimate. And it is notorious that a number of physicists today echo the creed that Einstein used, in varying forms, to express his sense of "religion."

> The most beautiful thing we can experience is the mysterious. It is the source of all true art and science. He to whom this emotion is a stranger, who can no longer pause to wonder and stand rapt in awe, is as good as dead: his eyes are closed. This insight into the mystery of life, coupled though it be with fear, has also given rise to religion. To know that what is impenetrable to us really exists, manifesting itself as the highest wisdom and the most radiant beauty which our dull faculties can comprehend only in their most primitive forms—this knowledge,

---

6. John Wheeler, quoted in *Between Quantum and Cosmos*, ed. Wojciech Hubert Zurek et al. (Princeton: Princeton University Press, 1988), 10.

7. John Polkinghorne, *Faith, Science, and Understanding* (New Haven: Yale University Press, 2000), 166, and "The Quantum World," in *Physics, Philosophy and Theology: A Common Quest for Understanding* (Vatican City: Vatican Observatory, 1988), 333–335.

this feeling, is at the center of true religiousness. In this sense, and in this sense only, I belong in the ranks of devoutly religious men.[8]

Werner Heisenberg recalls a time when four future Nobel Prize–winning physicists (Pauli, Dirac, Bohr, and Heisenberg) sat discussing Einstein's religious views, revealing that they'd all given some thought to the subject.[9] And Karl Popper recalled that "I learned nothing from Einstein directly, as a consequence of our conversations [in the 1950s]. He tended to express things in theological terms, and this was often the only way to argue with him. I found it quite uninteresting."[10]

Physicist Leon Lederman in *The God Particle* also complains that in recent years the last few pages of popular treatments of physics or cosmology, even by prominent scientists, are "always philosophical, and the Creator almost always appears."[11] He lacks sympathy with such sentiments and doubts their seriousness. But he is right that many find the language of religion suggestive when dealing with things at the extremes of either the cosmic or the atomic level. Their expressions of astonishment and humility remind one of Rudolf Otto's classic description of the numinous experience, in his *The Idea of the Holy*. Their awe has to do with "strangeness" (a common expression), the surprise of counter-intuitive aspects, the ingenuity and even wit that seem embedded in things. It all hints at something personal and purposive behind that which we still call "creation."

Within cosmology, the obvious problem for religion used to be humanity's microscopic scale in relation to the unimaginable size of our universe. It is easy to describe the universe in terms that reduce the human subject to perfect insignificance. Religion accordingly seems childish. Recent knowledge, however, has made us wonder what size has to do with significance. We are led to believe that at the Big Bang everything that would become the universe was a mere point, if that is

8. Henry G. Leach, ed., *Living Philosophies* (New York: Simon and Schuster, 1931), 6.

9. Werner Heisenberg, *Physics and Beyond* (New York: Harper and Row, 1971), 82–92.

10. Adam Gopnik, "The Porcupine," *New Yorker* (1 April 2002), 92.

11. Leon Lederman, *The God Particle* (Boston: Houghton-Mifflin, 1993), 409.

meaningful at such a moment. We also read that humans are something like halfway between the largest and smallest "things" in the present universe and that each single person of the 5-plus billion of us has a higher level of organization and richness of experience than a thousand galaxies.[12] All this seems to give humans something like a front-row seat for the cosmic drama.

Beyond that, as Polkinghorne puts it, "The most remarkable event following the big bang, of which we have knowledge, has been the universe's becoming aware of itself through humanity—the event that . . . has made science possible."[13] When cosmologist Steven Weinberg famously wrote that "the more the universe seems comprehensible, the more it also seems pointless," we must wonder what he meant.[14] For the universe to become *aware of itself* might strike us as quite incredibly interesting. For the beings that embody the universe's self-awareness to take a hand in their own evolution, first culturally and now through genetic engineering, is even more astounding.

Leaving aside any theological reflection, the fact that science itself has "evolved" out of *our* matter, matter that was not originally even organized in atoms, might strike some as an invitation for religious wonder. To see all this as uninteresting or pointless raises the question of where the notion of "interesting" came from.

We also discover that one of the so-called Anthropic Coincidences that scientists think made biological evolution and intelligence itself possible is precisely *the present size of the universe*. That is, there could not be intelligent life if the cosmos were any smaller than it is. They think it has taken this long an expansion in order to produce and distribute the carbon that is the basis for intelligent life. As Stephen Hawking points out, "If the rate of expansion one second after the Big Bang had been smaller by even one part in a hundred thousand million million [sic] it would have recollapsed before it reached its present size."

---

12. Ian G. Barbour, *Religion in an Age of Science* (London: SCM, 1990), 147.

13. Polkinghorne, *Faith, Science, and Understanding*, 188.

14. Steven Weinberg, *The First Three Minutes* (New York: Basic, 1977), 149. Weinberg later allowed that "people can grant significance to life by loving each other, investigating the universe, and doing other worthwhile things": Gregg Easterbrook, "Science and God: A Warming Trend," *Science* (15 August 1997), 893. But he did not justify the terms "grant," "significance," or "worthwhile."

Stars and planets would therefore not have developed, within which the elements formed that made intelligent life possible. And if the speed had been greater by one part in a million, it would have expanded too fast for those stars or planets to form.[15] Thus nature could not have transcended itself as it has, in humans who parade their modesty.

All of this about size proves nothing, of course. It is only offered to neutralize objections to religious consciousness as a lack of realism in the face of a staggering universe.

⌒

The discovery of dozens of these Anthropic Coincidences in the last generation has given such religiously charged questions a place within science itself. It means that not all cosmic wonder ends in mute astonishment. Actual discussion has been generated among physicists over these constants, which opens toward issues of cosmic purpose. Scientists recognize over thirty different parameters of our universe (and the number continues to grow) that are within the frightfully narrow ranges necessary for any conceivable life to develop at any time in the history of the universe.[16] Added together, they reduce the element of chance to nothing. It is hard to pose as nonchalant in the face of evidence that the universe seems to have had life in mind from the beginning. As physicist Freeman Dyson puts it: "The more I examine the universe and the details of its architecture, the more evidence I find that the universe in some sense must have known we were coming."[17] In the words of physicist John Wheeler, we are not simply "adapted to the universe. The universe is adapted to Man."[18]

Under ever-so-slightly-different initial conditions a classical universe—with defined objects existing at distinct locations and a well-defined concept of time—would not have emerged. Rather, there would have been a "smeared-out world" in which one would have to know everything to know anything. Science, as partial knowledge, would not

15. Quoted in Barbour, *Religion in an Age of Science*, 135; Hugh Ross, *The Creator and the Cosmos* (Colorado Springs: Navpress, 1993), 109.

16. Ross, *Creator and the Cosmos*, 111–112.

17. Quoted in Barbour, *Religion in an Age of Science*, 136.

18. John Wheeler, in John D. Barrow and Frank J. Tipler, *The Anthropic Cosmological Principle* (Oxford: Clarendon, 1986), vii.

have been possible under those conditions, if scientists are looking for something to be thankful for.[19]

When secular universities began, scientists were viewing human life as an accident. Recent recognition that if any of those fundamental and inexplicable physical "constants" (Planck's constant, the speed of light, the gravitational constant, the unit of electrical charge) were any different, intelligence could not have evolved, has changed that. Insofar as it makes sense to speak of the "initial conditions" at the Big Bang, they had to be just what they were if life was to be possible, and scientists have no theory of why they were just what they were. Einstein was among those who was interested in "God's" degree of choice in fixing these natural constants.[20]

The way that some get around this astonishment is to postulate an infinite number of quantum universes, embodying all possible physical conditions. Nobody takes that seriously when the subject is that Infinite Monkey who is typing *Hamlet*. It would seem more sensible just to be thankful that there is at least one universe that was designed to produce us.

Since science is now infinitely beyond public understanding and is generally taken (or rejected) on faith, science fiction becomes part of the unacknowledged curriculum on campuses. The picture of science it offers may remind us more of religious pilgrimage than of a laboratory. And the science involved is physics, not parapsychology, as I. P. Couliano observed:

> Curiously enough, a confirmation of the possibility—theoretical rather than practical—of otherworldly journeys has come not from psychological disciplines, but from hard science. Physics and mathematics are to be held responsible to a large extent for the return of interest in mystical ways of knowledge. They have opened up new perspectives

19. Paul Davies, *The Mind of God: The Scientific Basis for a Rational World* (New York: Simon and Schuster, 1992), 159. Stephen Hawking, among others, wonders about the very concept of initial conditions, in his consideration of a quantum cosmology (ibid., 62).

20. Polkinghorne, *Faith, Science, and Understanding*, 179.

by asserting that this visible universe is only a convention based on our perception, and that wonderful, unimagined worlds are hidden in tiny particles and perhaps even in the familiar space surrounding us. . . . Through science fiction, representations of other worlds have reached an unprecedented expansion, not coordinated by any basic world view.[21]

Even the beloved "special effects" technology of movies can be used to encourage religious experience. Worshipers have always used technologies in their activities, involving musical instruments, artistic illusion, vestments, colored light, and incense, which become "sacred" as they are absorbed in the cult. Whether it is entertainment or religion depends on the effect of the experience rather than the intentions of those producing it. Even the cynicism of movie producers would not necessarily block such effects, any more than the possible skepticism of medieval architects or sculptors has blocked the devotion of generations of worshipers.

We are not used to thinking of biological evolution as religiously suggestive, since it has raised such alarm among theologians and believers. But it now appears that evolution itself would depend on such design as seems implied in the Anthropic Coincidences.[22] And there are additional vital coincidences that are specific to our solar system as well as to the cosmos more generally.[23] So naturalism could well feel on the defensive these days.

Skeptics have challenged Anthropic enthusiasts to say what the existence of human life proves about the universe that the existence of, say, sulfur doesn't prove. Why does human existence seem to raise the issue of theism when other natural products don't? Of course it is because it raises that question of intelligence—or an Intelligence—in a larger sense. If we exhibit personality, that means *there is personality in the universe* of which we are a part. The presence within nature of a

21. I. P. Couliano, *Out of This World: Otherworldly Journeys from Gilgamesh to Albert Einstein* (Boston: Shambhala, 1991), 12, 29–30, 234–235.

22. Howard J. Van Till, "The Creation: Intelligently Designed or Optimally Equipped," *Theology Today* 55 (1998): 358–362.

23. Polkinghorne, *Faith, Science, and Understanding*, 66–77.

consciousness of nature, however it developed, is more remarkable than the presence of sulfur. Modesty should not obscure the fact that we make the universe a great deal more interesting.

Biologist Stephen Jay Gould denied that the Anthropic Coincidences are religiously suggestive because they fall short of an "argument for God's existence."[24] But the religious sense (as opposed to theological explanation) has no interest in proofs. Proof means the power to force others to agree, by an appeal to logic, facts, and shared assumptions. That is the way of science, but it is out of place in religion.

A sense of the fantastic surprise of life, and of intelligent life, may not be exactly a part of science. But the odds against life are the same odds against science ever coming into being. Those who want to contemplate how science itself survived those odds will be engaged in a religious enterprise.

The desire of some religious believers to have their religious epiphanies or doctrines recognized within academic science—to give the purposes of creation a place within it, for instance—is misguided; it is a category mistake. Religion would be swallowed into science. Rather, they might think of ways to incorporate our understanding of science within a religious framework. We could, for example, begin to see the history of science as part of the religious history of humanity.

There are two common approaches to the project of getting science and religion together, and they seem equally unpromising. One is to begin from a physicalist theory of matter, assert the derivation of all human characteristics from it, and invite theologians to find a point at which to penetrate this fortress. Half-hearted allusions will be made to quantum mechanics and indeterminacy, perhaps. The opposite approach is to begin from descriptions of the Absolute as omnipotent, omniscient, eternal, creative, loving, and then to wonder how those attributes would be compatible with human freedom or divine providence, within some notion of ordinary "nature." It is hard to imagine a bridge that could connect these parallel universes.[25]

To start from the middle, the mystery of the human, would make

---

24. Stephen Jay Gould, *Rocks of Ages: Science and Religion in the Fullness of Life* (New York: Ballantine, 1999), 218–220.
25. A theology called "panentheism" was once propounded as such a bridge, principally by Alfred N. Whitehead and Charles Hartshorne.

no such theoretical pretensions as these two approaches. But our positivistic and hermeneutical methods need to find ways to talk to each other. This discourse will at least have the advantage of connecting with experiences that are determinative for most of us. Universities will seem more interesting when they regain the aspect of discovery. For a century now, universities have allowed science to comment on religion, without encouraging a problematizing of science itself. We are at a pivotal moment, however. Our biggest questions today have more to do with our uses of knowledge than with its acquisition. Accordingly, we may expect to see science become the background, while questions of how we use our knowledge reveal how we define the human. One can imagine a future in which science serves religious ends, when our biggest questions concern a good life, a good society, and how to care for nature. All questions that suggest a dimension of ultimacy.

Nature has long been nominally defined as that which is indifferent to man. Cosmological and evolutionary doctrine themselves are allowing us to question that and are becoming religiously suggestive. Scientists themselves are becoming more frankly self-reflective. The history and philosophy of science is making us critically aware of the categories that shape scientific observations and facts. Thus, science need no longer seem the rival of the human and the personal. The university can take advantage of this opportunity, but will risk losing its audience if it cannot speak to such concerns or is seen as censoring them.

7

Teaching *about* Secularism, or Teaching Secularism?

One of the notable secularizing decisions of the U.S. Supreme Court was the 1963 *Abington Township School District v. Schempp* ruling, which only allowed tax-supported schools to teach *about* religion. Meaning, of course, that government schools could not directly *teach religion* in the sense of encouraging belief. Teaching about religion, of course, "relativizes" or marginalizes it. It teaches children to see religion from the outside, from some perspective that is thought to transcend it. The Supreme Court recognized this in stipulating that the teaching of religion must be "part of a secular program of education." This would tend to undermine the claims of any particular religion, although perhaps it was meant to give children an appreciation of religion in general, whatever that is.

Back in those days it was usual among intellectuals to think of the secular as the natural and as humanity's common destiny. By contrast, religions seemed divisive and doubtful and were expected to fade. Nowadays it is not so clear that this is happening. And since that date, scholars have begun to recognize that secular rationalism itself is not a neutral, absolute position, rising above all faith commitments. Secularism is seeming more and more like a stage within history, rather than its final goal. For it is recognized that rationalism and science themselves are based on shifting intellectual foundations and that there are no self-validating principles at the basis of all thought.

The result of these realizations is that we can now problematize secular rationalism itself.[1] We can see it as one way of thinking among others, one of those "traditions of inquiry" we've been mentioning.[2] We could describe its history, its assumptions, its methods, and the institutions that support it, as if it were a particular historical stage rather than our ultimate destiny.

So in principle, universities could teach "about" secularism as easily as they can teach about religion. For many years universities and the public schools have been teaching secularism in the sense of indoctrination and requiring the adoption of its assumptions.

Recently, however, our courts have become more sensitive to the rights of students not to be imposed upon by the government's schools. They have heard about multiculturalism and postmodernism, which insist that thinking is culture-specific. They are beginning to understand that there is no transcendent perspective which can arbitrate between those viewpoints. As philosopher Thomas Nagel put it, there is no "view from nowhere in particular."[3]

If the university's goal is to increase our knowledge of ourselves, then clearly it should be teaching about secularism, instead of just teaching secularism. For if it is one worldview among many and not a neutral position, it could become an "established ideology" like the established religions of old, with all the temptations of an unquestioned power.

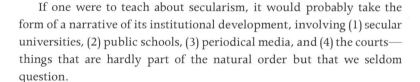

If one were to teach about secularism, it would probably take the form of a narrative of its institutional development, involving (1) secular universities, (2) public schools, (3) periodical media, and (4) the courts—things that are hardly part of the natural order but that we seldom question.

First, the course would have to define several terms. "Secularization" means, in the first sense, the separation of religion from other

1. Martin E. Marty, *Religion and Higher Education* (Columbia: University of Missouri Press, 1989), 4.
2. Alasdair MacIntyre, *Whose Justice? Which Rationality?* (Notre Dame: University of Notre Dame Press, 1988), and *Three Rival Versions of Moral Inquiry* (Notre Dame: University of Notre Dame Press, 1990).
3. Thomas Nagel, *Mortal Questions* (Cambridge: Cambridge University Press, 1979), 208.

aspects of life and thought.[4] "Secularity," then, would be the final state of that process, when our institutions and our thinking are indifferent to religion. But if we used the phrase "secular society," we would need to recognize the ambiguity in the term "society." It can mean either the framework of social structures or the persons who are fitted into these structures. It is possible that the structures or rules of society can be entirely secular while the population is largely religious (as seems to be the case in the United States today). For the secularization of thinking is the last stage of a much longer process, and may never go much farther than it has, or it might even be reversed, as seems to have happened sometimes.

Finally, the word "secularism" means something else again. It is the determined effort to *keep* religion marginalized, to complete secularization and enforce it. Secularism, then, is an ideology, and a course on secularism will indicate that in the past century there was a sizable effort in this direction that had only mixed success.

SECULAR UNIVERSITIES

We've already indicated the difficulties our universities are having, restricted as they are by the stipulations of secularist rationality. We have said that they have failed to fulfill their original hopes and are not offering leadership to American society. They may be giving in to the pressures to follow student interests, which center on employment, and to the pressure of legislators for some practical return on the state's support. We would now be hard-pressed to find a distinctive view of life or culture being promoted by the curriculum. In short, the momentum of their secularism has waned.

Richard Posner's *Public Intellectuals: A Story of Decline* comments on the recent decline of the elite leadership universities once embodied. In his view, the public contribution of academic and other intellectuals to our social debates is "becoming less distinctive, less interesting, and

---

4. C. John Sommerville, "Secular Society/Religious Population: Our Tacit Rules for Using the Term 'Secularization'," *Journal for the Scientific Study of Religion* 37 (1998): 249–253.

less important." Think tanks are becoming the conservative counter-weight to the liberalism of universities, resting on private money, free to pursue unpopular topics, and clustered around Washington.[5]

The marketplace has broken the dominance of academic liberalism over the media and now supports a growing number of conservative columnists. New media outlets are breaking ranks with journalistic culture, finding that there are profits to be made in attacking the "liberal media." This is jarring to those who have long thought that the liberal media was the antiestablishment.

Other elites are feeling beleaguered. In chapter 1 we saw that scientists such as Edward O. Wilson and Stephen Jay Gould show some alarm when science is treated merely as a servant rather than as a metaphysic or ideology. Americans think highly of science, of course, but don't see that this requires them to ignore religion. On the other hand, voices sympathetic to religion, like those of philosophers Charles Taylor, Mary Ann Glendon, Hilary Putnam, Paul Ricoeur, and John Milbank seem to challenge academic secularism from within. This may not be seeping through to the student body in any conscious way, but we can hardly miss our students' attitude that they have a right to their own views—after graduation, anyway.

In 1963 historian Richard Hofstadter published his widely studied *Anti-Intellectualism in American Life.* He had been dismayed at Dwight Eisenhower's 1952 election victory over the academy's choice of Adlai Stevenson. It seemed a repudiation of a generation of Democratic rule, "during which the intellectual had been in the main understood and respected." His hopes had been lifted at the election of John Kennedy in 1960.[6] But the scene has altered greatly since then, as university intellectuals' influence could now hardly be identified as such in American public life.

5. Richard A. Posner, *Public Intellectuals: A Study of Decline* (Cambridge, MA: Harvard University Press, 2001), 3, 6–7, 35.

6. Richard Hofstadter, *Anti-Intellectualism in American Life* (New York: Alfred A. Knopf, 1963), 4–5.

PUBLIC SCHOOLS

Tracing the failure of secularism within the public schools might center on the triumph of tolerance. Tolerance is part of the emphasis on diversity or multiculturalism in the curriculum. It was stimulated by a greater sensitivity to civil rights and to a widening immigration. In rejecting a single model of Americanization it embodied a secularist impulse. But tolerance may now be turning against secularization. Immigrants, for example, may very well be more religious than the native-born.

Toleration grew out of relativism, recognizing that the views of others related to their forms of life. It was embraced as a means in the search for a many-sided truth. But as truth seems to recede ever farther into the distance, tolerance has become an end in itself. This may work against a secularist worldview: for if the primary goal is tolerance, teachers may have a harder time squelching the ideas that students bring to school with them. To constrain discussion there would need to be something like rationalism to impose settled reference points. Now, teachers can only silence religious expressions by referring to the respect due to other religions. They may frown down unwelcome views, but that cannot be as effective as the arguments of a more confident age.

Courts are watchful of public education, trying to ensure that it respects the views of minorities. But they are beginning to realize that they have been promoting only the freedoms of secularist students and parents. There are hints of something new when they rule in favor of those students who exercise freedoms of speech and assembly for religious purposes. Student religious clubs may be resurrecting a bit of what school chapel attendance once accomplished. We find it curious that colleges and even some state universities once required chapel attendance, until secularism ended that. But at the very least, it could have reminded students the limits of our knowledge and that choices should be made in the light of one's highest wisdom. There is little that does that in universities these days. Independent schools, home schooling, or even the club life of public schools could increasingly perform something of that function.

The downward trajectory of secularism can also be seen in the abandonment of efforts to mold children's minds, bodies, and spirits, as educators once liked to say. Schools once required shop and home economics, physical education, speech, and languages. Students were forced to sit through performances of mature art in hopes that they would pass the threshold of appreciation. This has changed dramatically in the last couple of generations, as the curriculum narrows to job skills. Efforts to introduce young people to an adult culture have became apologetic. What students now learn is that the main standard is personal interest. And as for that, the commercial media are more powerful guides than their teachers.

In the late nineteenth century, educators hoped to spread a secondary education that had more cultural content than even universities insist on today. But that lasted only so long as high schools served a small percentage of the population. Secularism worked well enough in a world that was still elitist, depending on the brightest to blaze the trail. But in the 1930s and 1940s, John Dewey and others took a chance when they promoted a kind of cultural democracy and progressively lowered the educational bar. When everyone has a vote in philosophy as well as in politics, secularism will become only one option.

PERIODICAL MEDIA

Then there's the story of the media. In a secularist society the communications media take the place of tradition. The press, and especially the periodical press, were expected to break the power of entrenched error. They would keep ideas in play so that reason would be unconstrained. Religion was expected to lose out because it lacked the means of change and development that modernity depends on.

What has happened, we now realize, is that daily media have driven the more substantial media out of circulation. Serious books cannot compete with news. Dailiness deconstructs a culture once enshrined in the universities. It does so in order to market "news product" with no shelf life at all, the paradigm of planned obsolescence. And since capitalism requires that money find its most fruitful use, the news industry is now more about entertainment than enlightenment. This is not good for elite secularism.

Of course, the output of books is higher than ever. The number of new U.S. book titles each year is an unimaginable 50,000 titles. The upshot is that very few make any impact at all. They do not contribute to the vigorous debate that rationalism envisioned. Rather, we seem satisfied with the one big story of the day, and we may imagine that we are "informed" for having heard it. So the hope of a progressively more enlightened populace seems increasingly unrealistic. Some figures indicate that serious news consumption in the United States is falling faster than church attendance.

THE COURTS

The courts may be seen as a fourth pillar of secularism. That narrative begins in the mid-twentieth century, when the U.S. Supreme Court first posited a "wall of separation" between "church" and state. The difficulties in sorting that out within the public schools has led to inconsistencies so obvious that they are now prompting a reaction. Legal scholars are pointing out that judges shelter plaintiffs from the use of religious terms even outside of instruction, while refusing to shelter those who objected to the imposition of New Age assignments. Nonreligious children were said to be impressionable and vulnerable in cases involving religious invocations, whereas religious children whose beliefs were directly attacked were told to get used to it. Courts argued that exposing children to religious texts would have an impermissible effect but that "mere exposure" to antireligious texts will have no effect. Students have been forced to read texts questioning religious views, without a right of excusal, while religious books have been removed even from school library stacks. Law review articles have begun commenting on the absurdities involved in this secularizing campaign.

The view that government schools are constitutionally required to be neutral rather than secular is now out in the open. Warren Nord's *Religion and American Education* shows that the Supreme Court has held that the First Amendment requires not just neutrality between religions, but also between religion and nonreligion. Nord's own conclusion is that "neutrality *requires* the integration of religion into the [public school] curriculum," since he sees it as essential to the study of culture, history, politics, society, economics, and the uses of science.[7]

But teaching *about* religion, as Nord suggests, would not achieve neutrality without teaching about secularism too. For the public should be aware of the ideological nature of secularism, which imposes a particular way of life and defines a stage within history. In short, secularism can now be seen as a narrative—a story with a beginning and presumably an end—and not the all-embracing myth that it once seemed to be.

Neither teaching about religion nor teaching about secularism will be easy, given the training our teachers have received and the difficulty of thinking outside our cultural paradigms. This can be seen in their failure to actually teach cultural diversity, as opposed to simply disparaging majority culture. But if we could get a perspective on the present state of secular culture, we would be surprised at how deeply religion is still embedded in our thinking on many subjects.

The public has so far supported our government's suspicion of private education, from fears of social and religious division. They are remembering a day when the common school tried to bring Americans together in a common culture, but forgetting its present mandate to undermine such a culture, leaving only what is compatible with liberal capitalism. People who would not tolerate a government monopoly over news support an effective state monopoly over education. They have not yet seen that censorship is imposed not by parents but by school districts and publishers who can suppress any views they think outlandish. Given our federal system, however, one expects vouchers to have a chance to justify themselves at the level of states and for independent schools to test the secularist monopoly over education.

One possible end to the story of secularism has already gone into the history books, in the collapse of world communism. A study of the

7. Warren A. Nord, *Religion and American Education: Rethinking a National Dilemma* (Chapel Hill: University of North Carolina Press, 1995), 245.

reasons for its ideological and spiritual failure should look at the similarities as well as the differences between Russian and American secularism. It could include a consideration of the often humane hopes that involved Americans in the communist effort during our Great Depression, as well as the forces that defeated most communist governments.

Sociologists of religion have only begun to give attention to the study of secularization. So far, they have been concentrating on what is happening to religion instead of what is happening to secularism. Religion still offers their baseline or default values. Next, they will need to study generations raised without exposure to religion, to see what sense they are making of life.[8]

At a more impressionistic level, a recent book entitled *The Twilight of Atheism*, by professor of history and theology Alister McGrath, argues that aggressive or ideological atheism has peaked and is in decline. He supposes that is because arguments are not as compelling as imagination in forming our convictions. We seem to need to be able to visualize our basic reality. The Soviet Union's part in this drama could be of first importance, offering our most obvious visualization of atheism in its nightmarish material and mental failure.[9] McGrath learned this principle from Nietzsche, of all people. The question before us is who can provide a new vision for the future.

NOTE: THE LEGAL ISSUE IN RELIGION AND HIGHER EDUCATION

As we all recognize, our tax-supported agencies must be careful not to impose religious views on the public. Besides the issue of freedom, even religious sympathizers recognize the deadening effect that imposing dogma generally has, whether it is religious or Marxist. So we need to say something about the legal constraints that might be encountered in problematizing the secular or entertaining religious perspectives within

8. See my review of Steve Bruce's *God Is Dead: Secularization in the West*, in *Journal for the Scientific Study of Religion* 42 (2003): 305.

9. Alister McGrath, *The Twilight of Atheism* (New York: Doubleday, 2004), 48, 149, 174, 186–187.

public universities. We began the chapter with a reference to a landmark decision which stated that, even at the primary level, it was proper to teach about religion. But that is not at all what I have been arguing for.

The Supreme Court in 1963 could not imagine that religion might make an essential contribution to intellectual debate. They were only accommodating the urge to have schools inform children about what people had once believed. And perhaps to let citizens feel that their views were being given some public acknowledgment. It would not have occurred to the nine justices that secularism would come up short and need help from religious perspectives. But that is the possibility that I am trying to raise—not just that religious people feel marginalized by elite disdain but that the secularist impulse has failed in some areas.

So the question before us is close to that of whether religious arguments are proper in political debate in a democracy where not everybody is religious. The Supreme Court has sometimes acknowledged that adults are not like children and do not need such elaborate protections. In *Lee v. Weisman* (1992), for instance, they admitted that grown-ups were not as "susceptible to peer pressure" as adolescents. Their prohibition of commencement invocations in that decision was not to be a precedent to attack legislative prayers and other suggestions of a national piety. College students may fit the category of adults in this regard, though it is hard to predict how nine justices might feel on a given issue.

Our academic culture tries to make a point of respecting students' privacy, and we are used to thinking of religion as almost the essence of privacy. But we have been arguing that religion can be relevant to our most challenging intellectual issues as well. And if the point of university courses is to show students how to think about certain subjects, that seems to demand that religious perspectives be considered on their merits. To be sure, there are subjects where it is necessary to adopt a particular intellectual discipline. That is especially true of technical and scientific subjects. This is not where religion faces its greatest challenges or can make its greatest contribution.

So we are mainly talking about raising and "considering" religious views or concepts, heuristically or suggestively. Religions generally recognize that they do not depend on, or profit from, "proving" things. Proof is an exercise of power that religion no longer feels comfortable with. Religions don't think that "faith" is a weak word. In the arena of life, faith is easily the equal of proof. For a religion to offer proofs can be taken as a sign of bad faith, of a loss of confidence, because religion does not need to elicit complete agreement to make an impact. It offers perspectives, possibilities, narratives, concepts. In doing so it seems unlikely to fall afoul of the prohibition against "establishing" a religion. People should be free to seriously consider all manner of views; anything short of that would hardly be education.

And there is more to the issue of "establishment"; we need to revisit First Amendment jurisprudence to consider it. As you recall, there are two phrases in that Amendment concern religion. One says that no law may be made prohibiting the free exercise of religion, the other that no law can be made respecting an establishment of religion. For a long time it was thought that the former "clause" was *for* religion, the latter *against*. It was assumed that the former promoted the rights of the individual, while the latter restricted the rights of groups. These understandings produced inconsistent and irreconcilable bodies of case law. Some even thought that we needed two different definitions of religion, one narrow and substantive so as not to get in the way of our growing government, and the other broad and functional to protect our growing individualism.

Recently there has been a new interpretation of these matters. It holds that the "clauses" are not separate but have the same purpose. They both were to limit state involvement in religion. Obviously the state was supposed to respect the individual's free exercise. But the establishment prohibition was also to protect religious exercise against the federal state—in the form of a possible state church.[10] So both clauses are to safeguard free exercise, of individuals on the one hand and denominations on the other. This understanding could restore coherence to First Amendment jurisprudence, though it will require a tightening of the definition of religion so that it does not just mean conscience or privacy.[11]

The implication is that government must be neutral, among religions

---

10. Douglas Laycock, "Continuity and Change in the Threat to Religious Liberty: The Reformation Era and the Late Twentieth Century," *Minnesota Law Review* 80 (1996): 1087–1089.

11. C. John Sommerville, "Defining Religion and the Present Supreme Court," *Journal of Law and Public Policy* 6 (1994): 167–180.

but also between religion and nonreligion. Until recently, many legal philosophers took the view that government neutrality meant secularism. But as Nord has shown, the courts have already recognized that their neutrality may be between religion and nonreligion.[12] That way, power does not compromise any of these positions. The state does not itself act as a quasi-religious establishment.

Seen in this light, it should be illegal for tax-funded universities to eliminate religious perspectives simply because they are religious, if they otherwise seem plausible or convincing. That would be viewpoint discrimination, singling out religion alone and thereby committing an "impermissible classification" under the Due Process Clause of the Fifth Amendment. It would be different if we were talking about the primary grades, where students are too immature to exercise judgment. And it would be different if we were talking about technical fields, where utilitarian proofs can be decisive. But where religion can address the issues, and especially where they can help with them, there need not be a legal problem.

12. Nord, *Religion and American Education*, 161–168, 179, 249–259, 372.

8

LOSING A SENSE OF HISTORY

The story of the decline of the old Western Civilization course and the rise of something called World History represents no small change in the university. It may simply sound like a more broad-minded take on the curriculum, and some of my colleagues think of it that way. But it can be seen as the collapse of an entire understanding of education and its replacement by something different. Instead of trying to understand ourselves through our own history, the goal has become to distance students from themselves. Instead of an aid toward ethical judgment, history has become either a technical specialty or an exercise in moralizing. Once again, secularism was involved in replacing one with the other.

My professional life has involved teaching many semesters of Western Civilization, and I greatly enjoyed doing so. I was part of the Western Civ staff at Stanford around 1970, when that nationally recognized course was put out of business by marching students and wary administrators. Scholars did not risk anything to defend it. Where such courses still exist they continue to attract students, but they are rarely required. Many of my colleagues think that particular approach has been discredited, as they try to think what might replace it.

When I began in the profession, despite some debate on the subject, history was normally classified as a "humanities" subject. That is, it was meant to teach students what humans have been capable of—what they have built and what they have destroyed. As mentioned in chapter

2, however, the very notion of "human" has come to seem problematic and perhaps discredited by science and philosophical analysis. But fifty years ago history and literature were valued and even required because they were ways to learn about oneself.

How did our world become like it is? Why do we in the West perceive and react and think differently than people with other backgrounds? What events and ideas and persons have been important in shaping various periods, including our own? This view has been criticized as a "Whig" view of history, referring to those Victorian writers who saw all history as culminating in themselves. But that is a different thing from the view I'm expounding, which is that what we will find most meaningful will naturally be our own history. History should be "relevant," in the sense that any history course that doesn't teach you something about yourself is probably not worth taking. Antiquarians are interested in the past for its own sake, while historians are expected to have some purpose in studying it.

In the 1960s radical students talked a lot about "relevance" in the curriculum, and that talk was often ridiculed. But they had a point. We do not seem very sure that there is a point to history or literature courses now, beyond creating sympathy for the oppressed. This is the core of the moralizing we will discuss in the next chapter. The reduced concern for our own history has led to a restless revisionism that reflects our uncertainty about what the university is for.

Many groups are responsible for turning history into something less significant and something that hardly deserves to be required anymore. Administrators, scholars, advisers, legislators, and students all bear some responsibility for a hollowing-out of our curriculum. Legislators did not see that humanistic interests would contribute anything to the economy; administrators feared that students would grumble at subjects they were too young to appreciate; professors objected to teaching courses unrelated to their subspecialties; students didn't want to face parents who blanched at the job possibilities facing history majors.

The situation was partly caused by a change in the groups being educated. As universities ceased to be elite institutions after 1900 and began to serve mass society, they had a new role. In the Renaissance academies and universities, the idea of "liberal" arts meant an education for free men, who would not work for a living but who would be free to take on public responsibilities. Few students today are confident that they are destined for such positions and may resist the very notion of elites. But when secular universities began, educators thought they should at least teach what it was to be responsible citizens and sophisticated adults. Western Civ was one of the ways they tried to do it.[1]

In the late nineteenth century, Harvard president Charles W. Eliot decided to break the power of the classical curriculum, which centered on Latin and Greek literature. That had once seemed to sum up the wisdom of mankind and had been the core of Western education since the Renaissance. Now it seemed boring and decadent, and little more than a rite of passage. Yet Eliot's heralded elective system, copied widely, was a bit of a disappointment too, as his principle of unrestricted freedom seemed to dissolve all standards.

During World War I this became an issue for educators. They recognized a need for students to know why it was worthwhile to fight oppression. They asked themselves what in their culture and institutions could be worth sacrificing one's life for. Accordingly, the U.S. government sponsored a War Issues course as part of the officers' training program on campuses. It focused on the "evolution" of political freedom, democratic institutions, and rationality.

After the war Columbia University, which had been experimenting with a general European history course to replace the various national histories, continued this wartime initiative with a Peace Issues course. It was interdisciplinary, involving history, government, economics, and philosophy, and became popular even though it was required. Naturally it was elitist; the small percentage of the population that still dominated universities was expected to provide the nation's leadership. For those persons the history of high politics and philosophy seemed like practical training.

Meanwhile, the University of Chicago took a very different path

---

1. See Gilbert Allardyce, "The Rise and Fall of the Western Civilization Course," *American Historical Review* 87 (1982): 695–725, and Eugen Weber, "Western Civilization," in *Imagined Histories*, ed. Anthony Mulho and Gordon S. Wood (Princeton: Princeton University Press, 1998), 206–221.

toward curricular integration, creating required courses in "critical thinking," where logic and not narrative was the organizing principle. Their model for knowledge was therefore not history but social science. That approach did not prove as popular, even at Chicago, where it lost out to a more historically based general education curriculum. Textbook publishers spread these two approaches through the country, either in narrative histories, collections of source materials for discussion, or "problems" pamphlets.

The trouble with such courses stemmed from the effort to require them of all students. Through World War II and beyond, this was not a big issue, as students were perfectly aware of the threats that civilized standards were facing. But in the mid-1960s the situation changed. The West and its standards seemed to be discredited, especially by America's role in the Vietnam War and its poor record in domestic race relations. Many students revolted against values and requirements that had been generally accepted earlier but now seemed hypocritical.

By this time a much larger percentage of the American population found itself in college, and when they said "relevant" they seemed to mean learning about the surface of life. They showed more interest in histories of humble, everyday life in the past. Above all, they were afraid of glorifying powerful figures, or wars, or the upper reaches of diplomacy or politics where such fateful decisions were taken. Social history, cultural history, material culture, and issues of gender, class, race, and ethnicity brought the focus down to a level that had been neglected before. This popular history did not fit into the Western Civ approach, which was now stigmatized as the story of dead white European males.

Teaching both approaches did not seem practical, because the issue was in identifying introductory and required courses. If students only got a little history, which of these approaches would it be? Struggles over this decision were bitter because students representing previously neglected groups were entering the university with a sense of grievance. They had numerous accusations against the Western Civ course: it was incomplete, ethnocentric, and smug and told one what to think rather than training one how to think.

Of course, no history course covers more than a tiny fraction of what could be said on any subject; the most one course can do is to look for keys to the major developments. Incompleteness is a grievance only if the teacher gives the impression that it is complete. As to being arbitrary, again, the teacher should explain that the purpose of the course is to address the questions she thinks we are now most interested in, not to provide total historical recall. Since all courses are necessarily incomplete and arbitrary, the question is whether we can think of a better framework or better questions, and what makes them better.

The accusation of being provincial meant that the course only dealt with our civilization and not all the others. But you have to begin somewhere, and the Western Civ requirement assumed that would be with ourselves. Once you have some idea who you are, then your study of others will be more meaningful. The idea of beginning with one course that touches on all of history for all the cultures of the world is too absurd to contemplate, despite the fact that increasingly it is being done.

As for criticisms of ethnocentric smugness, we should note that such criticisms are characteristically Western. Far from discrediting Western Civ, this complaint actually embodies it, given that we are expected to treat the stranger, even the enemy, with charity. Yet while the West encourages others to be proud of their cultures, we disparage our own. Most cultures would not see any virtue in making their children overcome their ethnocentrism. In short, the usual criticisms of the required Western Civ course actually showed that its stress on Western values of charity, humility, self-criticism, and repentance had been successful.

Part of the objection to Western Civ was doubtless due to the notion that studying something is tantamount to glorifying it. It was easy to assume that studying the West was meant to justify its dominant position in the world, which has involved much oppression. We recognize it as oppression from the perspective of Judeo-Christian culture, which has become our second nature. The criticisms we have mentioned may show that the critics had not yet learned where their own ideas came from, taking them as self-evident.

What the university is now thinking of requiring are courses called World History. No doubt you have some idea of what World History means. That is the problem. If you think it means a brief survey of all the world's civilizations, you think like everyone else—students, parents, taxpayers, administrators, legislators; everybody but historians.

It is a measure of how out of touch academic historians are that they think they can define World History as they please and defy common usage. Historians know that there cannot be an intellectually respectable course that covers all of history for all of the world. That's not what they mean. But what they do mean is not yet clear, for they give a number of different meanings to this phrase. The phrase is in the public domain now, and thinking we can make it mean whatever we like will lead to trouble.

Academics need to coin different names for their project of globalizing history, like "comparative history" or "world encounters" or "borderlands history." This is because the public thinks that "world history" means everything-in-a-nutshell, so we won't have to take any more history courses. I'm talking about the students and the deans and legislators who will be interfering with it. There are plenty of high school World Civ courses that do that, so why can't a university?

In our overadministered universities we must consider what will happen to World History courses when deans get wind of them. They will decide that this is their showcase course, approve it for "general education" credit, and maybe even require it. Then it will cause major problems. Every minority, representing groups that have been ignored, will want to help design the course and have equal treatment. They will also want to help staff it, for how can they trust the course on everything important to their former oppressors? This was behind the 1960s demands for curricular change.

If deans approve and establish a World History requirement, the bulk of the faculty and their graduate student teaching assistants will be involved in teaching it, having to pretend to knowledge about all the major civilizations, their art, religions, economic systems, political organization and behavior, technologies, literatures, and social structures. Western Civ was subject to some of the same danger, but had at least some focus on a culture that, for better or worse, was still being absorbed through the media and the common school. We have not yet created a rationale for learning about others before we've learned about ourselves. The point in studying others is presumably to get another perspective on ourselves. That is what anthropology does in the study of alien cultures, and the study of the distant past can also make the present more strange and interesting. But where should we break into this hermeneutical circle?

The assumption that we should be studying someone else has become simply reflexive these days. You see it in Martha Nussbaum's discussion of the "humanity curriculum," mentioned in chapter 1. After quoting Socrates on self-examination, her whole book is all about knowing others—whether blacks, ethnics, women, or homosexuals. She complains that the University of Notre Dame has more courses on Ireland than on China or India.[2] Socrates would surely have understood that. We should not assume that students intuit their own traditions, remembering that most students' last brush with history was a course taught by a coach.

This, I think, is where secularism comes into the picture. From the time secularism began as an ideology, in the generation of Voltaire and Rousseau, it has promoted the project of destroying traditions. They and other Enlightenment authors liked to write from the perspective of Huron Indians or Persians or Chinese, to show how ridiculous European civilization could seem if you put your criticisms into alien terms. Calling bishops "shamans," the King of France a "pasha," and physicians "medicine men" helped readers achieve independence from an overbearing heritage. But it was one thing to break the crust over culture and another to create an amnesia that has left us homeless. Criticism has become such a settled habit that secularists cannot break it. The aim can go beyond disparaging our culture to destroying it. Since secularism aspires to transcend culture, it will want to require the new World History in place of Western Civ, not alongside it.

The Western Civ course was a reaction against too-rapid secularization. Educators at the beginning of the last century feared that students would not learn about their own roots or the nature of their threatened institutions. In designing the course, they could not ignore the fact that religion was central to the formation of Western Civiliza-

2. Martha C. Nussbaum, *Cultivating Humanity: A Classical Defense of Reform in Liberal Education* (Cambridge, MA: Harvard University Press, 1997), 272.

tion. They were only then beginning to learn how many of the political, social, cultural, and even economic forms that the *philosophes* took for granted had their origins in a specifically Christian culture.

The list of institutions flowing from this culture includes things we and our students take utterly for granted. The romantic tradition in literature and now in pop music, universities that combine scholarship and teaching, the restraint of power by law that grew out of the tension maintained between church and state, democratic institutions, political radicalism, capitalism, individualism, science—these aren't so native outside the Christian West. Even institutional secularization, so notably lacking in some traditions, was first sponsored by Western religious groups who wanted religion to maintain its independence from the earthly powers.[3]

That is just a start toward listing the ways that our social and cultural forms are associated with religion. Historians may disagree on the comparative weight to be given to religion and to other possible causes. And they may disagree on how beneficial these things have been. There are costs associated with every development, of course. But secularists use a moral objection to Western development to justify ignoring it, as if denying it our attention somehow diminishes it, when it only diminishes us.

In 2004 American society got a lesson in what we have done to the study of history. It involved two cultural events of enormous dimensions: the popularity of Dan Brown's novel *The Da Vinci Code* and the appearance of Mel Gibson's movie *The Passion of the Christ*. Interestingly, they both were primarily about Christian origins, showing the public's continued fascination with religion. The university showed it was not equipped to deal forcefully with the uproar over them.

Dan Brown's *The Da Vinci Code* was more than a book. It was an event, a phenomenon. People forgot that they had found it in the fiction section. What the public learned from it was almost entirely false, and

3. See C. John Sommerville, *The Secularization of Early Modern England: From Religious Culture to Religious Faith* (New York: Oxford University Press, 1992), for the way that various aspects of life and thought were freed from religious associations or control.

the episode showed two things about our universities. First, the most widely educated public in the world's history either could not spot the fraud or didn't care, and second, academics made no effort to alert the public when it was being overwhelmed. I can't help thinking that it passed without comment in the academy because it encouraged secularism instead of challenging it. For at the very same time, academics were much in the news for attacking Mel Gibson over his movie of *The Passion of the Christ*, with very little basis for their negative judgment.

I first heard of *The Da Vinci Code* when a student burst into my office to share her excitement about this thriller she had just read that had all this history in it. As I began reading, I could hardly believe it possible for a book to make so many obvious, and important, misstatements. Fiction has no responsibility to be true, but one doesn't expect historical fiction to be all false. Typically such novels fill the gaps in our knowledge with arresting and plausible details. Actually, there are reasons to think that Dan Brown at first intended his mistakes to be so obvious to sophisticated readers that they would wink back at him. On the first page, titled "Fact," he declares, "All descriptions of artwork, architecture, documents, and secret rituals in this novel are accurate." The most famous documents he mentions are the Dead Sea Scrolls; on page 234 he says that "these documents speak of Christ's ministry in very human terms," and he repeats that ten pages later. Actually, they are Old Testament documents for the most part, and pre-Christian. Most people know this. Is he making a joke?

On the other hand, Dan Brown makes a big point of his scholarly credentials, listing archives he visited. He includes long professorial discussions on the history of the Church. The novel is all about Truth (invariably capitalized), falsehood, secrets, proof, and disproof. His radical misinterpretation of church history is pushed pretty hard. In short, there is nothing to suggest that the book is all made up.

Historians would find the heart of the story around pages 230–234, where one professorial character explains that the Emperor Constantine imposed a whole new interpretation of Christianity at the Council of Nicaea in 325. That is, he decreed the belief in Jesus' divinity and suppressed all the evidence of his humanity. This would mean that Christianity won the religious competition of the Roman empire by an exercise of power, rather than by any attraction it exerted. In fact, the

Church won that competition before it had any power, when it was still under sporadic persecution itself. If you wanted to be cynical about Constantine, you would say that he chose Christianity because it had already won that competition, and he wanted to back a winner.

In the last year or so more than a dozen book-length refutations have appeared, documenting Brown's mistakes point by point. It is noteworthy that they are not by scholars at secular universities. But they must be continually jarred by Brown's offhand assertions. When he says that the Church executed 5 million witches in the Middle Ages, they might know that 5 million would be something like double the estimated population of England in the later Middle Ages—men, women, and children. It is 150 times larger than the standard guesses concerning this horror. If most of the witches were adult women, those European populations would have been in danger of going extinct. You don't need to go to an archive to check on these things; an encyclopedia would do.

So the book is a huge falsification of history, whose main point is that the Church has falsified history. A lot of readers are going to hear that there are some errors in the book, but they are likely to be forgiving. The focus of high school instruction for a century has been the more colorful and brutal aspects of medieval Europe. We would now be inclined to suspect courses that took another view. That other view is taught in universities, but no one would think of requiring such courses. It is an illustration of how otherwise educated people are encouraged to think that Western Civilization hardly deserves fair treatment.

It is unfair to hold Brown responsible for the astounding popularity of his book. After all, he didn't write a best-seller; he just wrote a book. The public made it a best-seller, and it's our fault if we mistake it for something substantial. Caught in his own popularity, he continues to argue the plausibility of his "interpretations," and there is no lack of reviewers who attest to his historical expertise. We have not heard from the universities yet.

Scholars have a stake in the truth of the historical record. Christianity put its stamp on our civilization in ways one would realize only by visiting the others. It is a civilization that threatens to engulf all other cultures, which can be a scary thought. And it has attractions that we unaccountably feel duty-bound to ignore. It fell to the maverick and skeptical sociologist Rodney Stark to point some of them out recently in his *The Rise of Christianity*, in his perverse hope to *épater les intellectuels*.[4]

The oddest thing about the *Da Vinci Code* phenomenon is to think that when secularists began to attack Christianity absolutely, in Voltaire's time, they thought that the truth was on their side, to use against the Church's legends. Now secularists countenance fabrications that verge on the bizarre. When one thinks of all the current movies and historical fictions that use similar deceptions, one is tempted to think that elite secularism is losing its nerve.

Our history department was never approached by anyone who wanted more expert opinion on the book, and we never thought to volunteer a presentation on it. We were busy educating our thousand history majors. Meanwhile, millions have now absorbed their ancient and medieval history from Dan Brown. He offered universities a golden opportunity for real enlightenment while we had the public's attention. Instead, the academy was belaboring Mel Gibson's use of the Gospels.

Scholars considered it important to warn the public against *The Passion*, but what was the problem exactly? Clearly, it was not a deliberate falsehood from start to finish, like *The Da Vinci Code*. For Gibson did not set out to reject the only historical sources scholars have for the events he treated. The scholars thought he should have.

Their most prominent spokesperson may have been Professor Paula Fredrickson of Boston University, who had written a recent book on the records of Jesus' trial.[5] In it, she presented very tentative speculation on the episode, and even admitted that she was reversing her earlier published views of these issues. But her tone when writing for the *New Republic* was totally different, ridiculing Gibson for taking something like her older position. Her current take on the subject seemed governed by journalistic concerns over anti-Semitism. She now thought that the Gospel accounts of Jesus' cleansing of the Temple must be mistaken,

4. Rodney Stark, *The Rise of Christianity* (Princeton: Princeton University Press, 1996).
5. Paula Fredrickson, *Jesus of Nazareth, King of the Jews* (New York: Alfred A. Knopf, 1999).

while the stories of the Palm Sunday procession must have been accurate. Why, since they have the same documentary pedigree? Perhaps because the former would have angered Jews and the latter would have angered Romans. And after all, it was the Romans who carried out the execution.

Journalists did not wait for her next book. With no more "proof" than that, they faulted Gibson for not fabricating an alternative that would be less offensive. Much was made of evidence that at other times Pilate had been more rigid. Historians deal with inconsistencies all the time, but it will now take a brave scholar to point out that there is no pressing reason to doubt the standard accounts, whose differences are trifling. Or to remind us that the evidence we have for the life of Jesus compares favorably with what we have for the emperor at the time, Tiberias.[6]

There is an obvious similarity between these two episodes. In each case academics have sided with secularist attacks on a religious tradition. When Dan Brown makes hash of the tradition, scholars are silent; when Mel Gibson innocently expresses it, we all hear about it. The historical gaffes that Gibson committed (having Eastern legionaries speak Latin rather than Greek, for example) do not begin to compare with Dan Brown's relentless and cynical falsifications. The two episodes remind us of the reaction to the attacks of 9/11, when journalists recruited academics to insist on the essential peaceableness of Islam, perhaps not as much to justify Islam as to forestall someone else's censure.

Older readers may remember Sir Kenneth Clark's television series called *Civilisation* which first aired in 1969. It was a major cultural event then, of a kind that is less and less frequent now. It was notable that Clark started his masterful survey of Western art and thought not with the Greeks or Romans, as one might expect. He began in the depths of the Dark Ages, when the Church struggled to fuse our worldview out of Christian and classical elements. Clark recognized that what went before is interesting, but it is not us.

---

6. A. N. Sherwin-White, *Roman Society and Roman Law in the New Testament* (Grand Rapids, MI: Baker, 1978), 187–188.

The prominence of the West in the world today is a grievance for many, and one can see their point. We may even share this grievance, yet we want to understand ourselves through our history. We owe it to our immigrant populations, especially, to explain what brought them here. To be sure, there was unpleasantness accompanying our drive toward liberty, democracy, enlightenment, science. For no advance comes without cost, unintended consequences, paradox. The question of what we don't like about ourselves is an important one. But a more important one is, who are we? An answer to that can come only from historical study born in humility.

9

MORALIZING AS A BAD HABIT

Secularizing the university has come to mean shying away from ethical judgments since these are apt to involve ultimate or religious standards. But one could not be around our secular universities for long without becoming aware of how much moralizing of their subjects goes on. It is so casual that one suspects that academics do not know where this moralizing is coming from, or how it is related to ethics. And they aren't always alert to how such moralizing, shallow as it sometimes is, contradicts the naturalism and relativism that is also present. It has become a confusing state of affairs.

Moralizing isn't quite the same as being moral. It's more like parading one's morality. Moralizing is blaming others, while ethics is examining ourselves. Moralizing makes students feel at home; it seems so natural. They would be more shocked to hear an entirely nihilistic or naturalistic view of culture or history. Although that may be the tendency of their professors' reasoning, they don't hear it in so many words.

Casual moralizing implies that our ethical stance is self-evident and assumes the currently fashionable values. Those who are offended by this and for some reason buck the moral fashion call it "political correctness." Rather than engaging in measured debate, each side is then tempted to escalate to accusations of "hate speech." Raising our consciousness on this issue might sharpen our sense of lost possibilities.

Moralizing at least indicates that we are moral beings, and unique within creation in that respect. Naturalism, by contrast, is the denial of specifically human values. Naturalism may not be fully acknowledged or articulated or even recognized by academics but is the closest thing to a philosophy that students will find on the premises. Intellectual and moral relativism, meanwhile, are now known as tolerance. It is the value that our secularist educational, entertainment, media, and judicial elites do most to articulate. So our philosophical tendencies are countered by a moralizing that is probably more potent for being simply assumed.

The idea of the secular university is not commonly thought to include a responsibility for moral education. Perhaps it did originally, back in 1900. But with the adoption of the fact/value distinction, universities have adopted a self-denying ordinance with respect to ethics. They are ethically committed against "imposing a morality" on students. But they cannot resist insinuating one, again suggesting that the notion of secularist education was a flawed concept from the beginning. Meanwhile, the formal instruction in ethics has become an exercise in intellectual discrimination or values clarification, which is not primarily to limit students' choice in this matter. Students may get the idea that they should not leave the course with their minds made up. Ethics becomes something a little removed from action or habit.

That is one difference that the presence of religion could make in the university. Religions call for a connection of mind and will, and they try to offer rationales for that connection. The problem the secular university sees with any religious rationale is that not everybody shares it. Moralizing aims directly at the will by presuming on the audience's existing values, in a drive toward creating a common mind.

There are some resources within the university, however, that can help it come closer to a conscious approach than it recognizes. I take my own field, history, as an example. History cannot help countering naturalism and relativism, as we shall see. Of course, given that history enrollments are declining and requirements for history are being abandoned, this would not be a very important point. But we should also recognize that historical approaches and "narrative" understandings are spreading beyond history departments.

If students did not feel morally engaged, they would have no interest in taking history courses. They want to be told who to side with in a historical situation, or to figure it out from the hints their instructors drop. Professors, too, would lose interest in their subject if they could not hint at the judgment of history. What could keep them going through a thirty-five year career better than moral indignation? Marxists cheer a triumph of the oppressed, nationalists hope for the triumph of their nation or culture, feminists trace how women have achieved their rightful place, the ecologically minded show why humanity will have deserved its fate.

Half a century ago there was an effort to break away from the moral tone that characterized traditional narrative histories. In the 1960s some thought went into trying to turn history from a "humanities" subject into a social science. That would mean that instead of seeing human life from the inside, we would view it from the outside. Instead of trying to understand human intentions, we would look for patterns of behavior. Instead of telling stories, historians would aim at statistical expressions of general laws of behavior. This would involve determinist assumptions and leave ethics behind. The effort is described briefly in Peter Novick's *That Noble Dream.*[1] The goal would have been objectivity—what we all can agree on, supposedly.

Social science history involved a lot of quantification and statistical effort. Historians tend to be high verbal, and I suppose this was what defeated this revolution. We are needlessly neglecting quantified approaches now. But the fact is that the profession as a whole has gone another way. It is now unashamedly narrative in its methods.

Using narrative as an intellectual method, and not just a mode of description, has important implications. Investigating the past through narrative leaves the humanity of our subjects intact, taking their moral character, their purposes, hopes, and values for granted as parts of the story and of its explanation. Narrative deals with persons, and not with

---

1. Peter Novick, *That Noble Dream: The "Objectivity Question" and the American Historical Profession* (Cambridge: Cambridge University Press, 1988), 392–400.

statistical abstractions or points on a scatter diagram. Microhistory, a recent fashion, is a perfect example of the desire to get down to the level of individual stories, where our sympathies are most fully engaged.

So narrative entails moral viewpoints. It implies that humans cannot be reduced to the usual terms of naturalism. Naturalism has also been attacked more directly of late, in critiques of sociobiology or evolutionary psychology. It is obviously true that humans function as the carriers of genes and work toward their survival, but there is no need to privilege that function over many other things we do; it doesn't have to be our defining characteristic.

Naturalism quickly exposes its shallowness when it tries to reduce the idea of the human to lower levels of analysis. When Stephen Jay Gould declared that "nature is amoral," he was in the middle of lecturing us (parts of nature, as he insisted) on our moral duties.[2] In chapter 2 we argued that the irreducibility of concepts like "responsibility," "wealth," "truth," "justice," "human rights," and "humane" all imply optimal human states and that if human categories had to be given up, most of the university should close down.

A half century ago, in *The Abolition of Man*, C. S. Lewis explained what a consistent adoption of a nihilistic naturalism would mean. If everything were really reduced to power (not just politics), those who achieved it would presumably use their knowledge to subjugate the rest of us. There would be no need for universities, whose existence implies *public* participation in knowledge and in its power.

How would all this figure in a history lecture? Say we wanted to explain Lincoln's assassination. No one would be satisfied with a doctor's statement that brain trauma was the only objective thing to say about the event. Or a physicist's comment that we're really talking about a collision of bullet with body tissue. Or an engineer's assurance that our subject was firearms. Only when we begin to consider human agency—a particular person, or a movement or ideology behind John

2. Stephen Jay Gould, *Rocks of Ages: Science and Religion in the Fullness of Life* (New York: Ballantine, 1999), 202.

Wilkes Booth—are we getting to our real questions. That is, historical explanations are only adequate when we get to a moral dimension.

Equally, it would be a mistake to continue by explaining Booth as a certain psychological type, as if that determined his action. We are not satisfied until we find the intentional and personal element in our stories, whatever else there is to consider. Of course, there is an outside to history too, in the objective circumstances of the event. But the inside is what we, as fellow humans, are really after.

Language itself turns against those who would reduce us to mechanistic, nonmoral terms. When Gould forgot to include us within his concept of nature, he showed how deeply he had absorbed the lesson that though humans are part of nature, they also transcend nature. So long as "human" is used unselfconsciously, it will entail purposes and narratives. It will raise the ethical point that people are not simply the means to someone else's ends. Universities have probably never been more sensitive to oppression and the belittling of others. Once we learn that persons are ends in themselves, it's not a lesson we can really forget, whatever our philosophies seem to require.

There is little resistance to this use of narrative in the secular university, despite its implicit ethical dimension. Peter Novick tells how some historians resisted the announcement of a "return of narrative" in the early 1980s, on the grounds that it would inevitably promote traditional or conservative views of human affairs.[3] But we notice that the critics were not objecting to an ethical emphasis; they just preferred different values. There was also resistance to Hayden White's philosophical works which seemed to say that history is a kind of fiction. He was simply likening narrative to the role of fiction in moral formation. Back in the 1970s White had to make his case for ethical engagement in difficult philosophical terms; now it seems to be taken for granted.

The divorce between history and social science is not final. We should continue to use objective and statistical data, since history will always have an outside as well as an inside. But we should also be aware that something strange is happening to the social sciences. They are

3. Novick, *That Noble Dream*, 622–623.

beginning to use narrative techniques in their research. Social scientists are using narratives to see how situations are constructed by participants, rather than how those situations appear in theory, objectified. Psychotherapy is also turning toward patients' stories and away from objectifying theories of behavior. Likewise, physicians who want to involve patients in their own treatment are taking an interest in their narratives. Medical research even has a journal devoted to the approach: *Literature and Medicine*. So narrative is informing the sciences themselves. And this will force them to listen for the ethical and religious considerations that make their patients human beings and not just bodies.

We have already drawn attention to the way science is now being understood through its narrative, rather than through a simple chronicle of discoveries. We used to think of science as the model of transcendent secular rationalism and therefore in some sense unhistorical. But it doesn't simply develop from an inner logic.[4] Michael Polanyi showed that single experiments could never be reduced to a formal algorithm but are irreducibly narrative in structure and description.[5] In short, human and moral considerations are involved in our understanding (our narrative) of science itself.

Originally, secular universities had no intention of questioning ethical concerns. They often announced their goal as the shaping of students' minds, bodies, and spirits. But as science became the model for all disciplines, they gave a decided priority to facts. Now we realize you can overdo that.

The humanities can also counter whatever threat an offhand moral relativism, sometimes called "tolerance," presents. Tolerance is a dominant value in academic culture. It truly is a moral value when the tolerance is for persons. But we have fallen into the habit of speaking of tolerance for ideas. That is not a moral position, but simply intellectual relativism.

4. E.g., see the discussion in Ian Hacking, *The Social Construction of What?* (Cambridge, MA: Harvard University Press, 1999).
5. Michael Polanyi, *Personal Knowledge: Towards a Post-Critical Philosophy* (London: Routledge, 1962), 49–53, 86–90, 162.

We see the confusion of these two senses of tolerance in the matter of campus speech codes, which have become a mark of the university's dogmatic secularism. Conservative critics like to point out the inconsistencies involved. University officials sometimes declare that they are tolerant of everything but intolerance. This stance depends on the assumption that tolerance for certain persons requires intolerance for certain ideas. This is how "tolerance" is used to stifle free speech.

The confusion comes from the assumption that a person's ideas are somehow intrinsic to their race, gender, or background and cannot change. This "essentialist" assumption holds that since they did not come to their ideas through rational means, it is unfair to suggest that they change their minds. It seems to follow that you cannot respect persons while attacking their views. The essence of moralizing is pity, whereas insisting on the "truth" of some position might create discomfort. Thus intellectual relativism is enforced in the guise of a moral position, as if ideas had rights. Actually, only persons have rights.

How could the study of history help counter this hypertrophy of relativism? How could academic history help actual values or virtues get past the tolerance patrol? One way would be by sympathetically presenting the values of the past, and presenting them as if they made sense. I have already given an example in chapter 5. The discussion of the conversion of the Anglo-Saxons to Christianity showed how self-evident both of those value systems seemed to the two sides in that face-off. Students expect some unpleasantness in the historical narrative. They expect religious leaders to be engaged in controlling activities and intellectual dogmatism. Students want to sympathize with those who were being evangelized. They may not realize that we acquired these sympathies from Jesus, who popularized the idea that religion goes bad when it is used in support of power systems.

But students find that it's not easy to take the pagans' side. These young agnostics' own notions of religion include moral and spiritual considerations, while the pagans treated religion as a way of ensuring good fortune in war and in fertility. My lectures have probably never made any converts to the warrior aristocracy's value system, the one based in honor. The students' own mentality is too Christian to allow it, and the university ought not be required to destroy their mentality on that account.

These two contrary systems were equally obvious to the different groups or, as we might say, "relative" to their different forms of life. But the corollaries of the two systems are dramatically different and challenge my students to exercise judgment. Given a moment to stare at the differences on a blackboard, students will realize that their choice has already been made. The pagan, aristocratic values that intrigued Nietzsche are not an option for us now.

It probably took the English several generations to absorb the Christian values preached by those monks. But they are so much a part of our students' minds now that they don't know there are others. Thus, a study of history can raise their consciousness about values, well beyond a simple appeal to tolerance.

Alasdair MacIntyre has argued that we do, in fact, judge between incommensurable positions.[6] Those who know only their own position may attack the right of others to argue against it. But those who have fully understood the different positions need not be too modest to express their judgment. They won't be able to argue it logically, because others may not share their breadth of view. As we say, there's no arguing about "taste." But they might hope that experience will someday open the other's mind.

(The same goes for artistic taste, another conversation-stopper around universities. Someone who knew both Beethoven and bluegrass could be justified in asserting that Beethoven was, well, superior. But she couldn't argue it except with others who shared a thorough understanding of both. This goes to the heart of Harold Bloom's theory of canon-formation, which does not turn on the exercise of *critical* power, but registers the triumphs of those authors who can force nascent literary traditions to make room for them. As he observes, however, ideological defenses of the canon are as objectionable as ideological attacks on it, both missing its evolutionary character.)[7]

$\backsim$

6. Alasdair MacIntyre, *Three Rival Versions of Moral Enquiry* (Notre Dame, IN: University of Notre Dame Press, 1990), 81.
7. Harold Bloom, *The Western Canon: The Books and School of the Ages* (New York: Riverhead, 1994), 16–19.

The moralizing that goes on in university courses assumes that the currently fashionable values are self-evident, among thinking persons. Actually exploring those moral fashions would indicate that they are relative, but also what they are relative to. Taken seriously, traditional religions could present a challenge for secular universities that have become unable to justify themselves for lack of practice. Without this challenge, the secular university becomes arbitrary and unconvincing in its moralizing.

While we're on the subject, we shouldn't forget that teachers are narratives in their own right. Ethics is modeled as well as taught. Thoughtfulness and concern and conviction may rub off on students. Cynicism, irresponsibility, and a debonair nihilism have more limited attractions. There are bound to be more temptations to be overbearing if your ideas have not been challenged recently.

One can hardly overestimate the moral instinct that animates our universities. In humanities departments it may seem that the university's patron saint these days is Nietzsche, the prophet of nihilism. But even his proponents seem determined to treat him as a moralist. A desire to help him unmask the power concealed within philosophy, science, religion, and even universities is evidently from a desire to shame us out of our oppressive ways.

Nothing wrong in that. Our critical schools aim at freeing the individual from the constraints of our politics, our society and culture, our literary forms, and language itself. Everyone from Marxists and the Frankfurt school to those in subaltern and queer studies show us how things look to victims. Again, this is in a Christian tradition, which promised deliverance from guilt, from the law, from sin, slavery, superstition, and the fear of death.

But the unmasking should not end too soon. Secularism itself may impose a fashionable moralizing. A deeper tradition of freedom includes what the Epistle of James paradoxically calls the "*law* of liberty," or what Jesus and Paul called the "*law* of love." This was presumably the freedom to follow another nature beyond one's partial desires. Thus we could be arguing ethically over what humans need besides freedom and tolerance.

10

HOW RELIGIOUS SCHOLARS
COULD CONTRIBUTE

Christians scholars have complained recently that they don't have a voice in the academy, or not as much as they should. Normally this is put as a matter of justice, since the great bulk of the American population identifies itself as religious while universities make a point of not recognizing any such point of view. Secularists, meanwhile, fear that whatever religious concepts remain would be very personal beliefs and merely divisive.

I have been making a different argument: that the secularism that looked vital and self-sufficient in 1900 has exhausted itself before reaching its goals of offering wisdom and leadership to American life. By limiting the university's attention to what we supposedly could all agree on—the objective or rational—secularism has not fulfilled our hopes. It has not become the cathedral of learning that was promised.

However, I must admit that if universities were to take any of this to heart and invite religious voices into the discussion, it would probably take a while for the response to emerge. A century in which religious voices were silent has taken a toll. What was the point of maintaining an intellectual and theological connection between religion and academics in the face of secular hegemony? Why bother translating those views into the terms of an increasingly alien discourse? Religious persons have other interests than "apologetics" and have concentrated on them, for better or for worse.[1]

All this has meant that for a generation or more, religion has seemed to be devoid of intellectual merit. Religious views on important questions have not developed and have become nearly invisible. The situation of just 150 years ago, as described in works like William Clebsch's *From Sacred to Profane America: The Role of Religion in American History*, can scarcely be imagined today.[2] Only in seminaries has there been institutional recognition for religious intellectualism. And it may be there that Christians will look for a revitalization of this activity.

Alasdair MacIntyre once wrote that we may need different universities representing the different approaches that seem justified.[3] Short of that, maybe each university could use at least three different philosophy departments. To those who have found themselves on the wrong side of our departmental battles, it must seem that he has something there. The triumph of secularism is not altogether due to its success in settling the questions before us, which can be exaggerated. Increasingly it seems to represent the exercise of institutional power. So at least we need a greater variety of faculty and an atmosphere freer of the prevailing self-censorship. In 1900 Western thought was dominated by the epistemological turn in philosophy, hoping to find objective truths that would speak to every aspect of our condition. Now we recognize that there are several "conversations" going on and different language games growing out of different "forms of life," science itself being one of these. Our multiversities themselves contain several of them. Professional education is not finding in the secularized humanities the resources to help them transcend their technical and utilitarian terms. I have been suggesting that religious and personalist vocabularies might bring new realism and interest to such subjects.

Welcoming religious viewpoints into university debates on issue involving human welfare would not instantly resolve anything. It might

1. See, for example, the criticisms of Mark A. Noll in *The Scandal of the Evangelical Mind* (Grand Rapids, MI: William B. Eerdmans, 1994).
2. William A. Clebsch, *From Sacred to Profane America: The Role of Religion in American History* (New York: Harper and Row, 1968).
3. Alasdair MacIntyre, *Three Rival Versions of Moral Enquiry* (Notre Dame: University of Notre Dame Press, 1990), 234.

even complicate matters, if different religious voices spoke in different dialects. But it might bring realism where ideas that are basically religious are present but not acknowledged as such. For I have argued both that the university is too secular and that it is not as secular as it thinks it is. In short, it is trying to enforce a secularism that has not been successfully argued as yet.

Still, if religiously Christian and Jewish scholars are allowed to be themselves in their academic roles, they will have to do a lot of thinking about how they might make a contribution. A few religious voices have been raised in more than protest. Historian George Marsden's *The Outrageous Idea of Christian Scholarship* does more than demand a place at the multiculturalist table. He thinks religion is not only an object of study or a set of dogmatic positions but offers perspectives on things generally. It is like secular faiths in that, "broadly understood, faith in something or other informs all scholarship."[4] Beyond his critique of the blinders of secularism, he suggests that it will be questions about the human where an opening to "faith-informed scholarship" is most relevant.

Two Christian scholars he might point to in this connection are Reinhold Niebuhr and Charles Taylor. The first volume of Niebuhr's *The Nature and Destiny of Man*, first published in 1941, is a model for Christian scholarship of one type.[5] It takes on leading philosophies and ideologies and subjects them to searching criticism. Then he shows how specifically Christian views seem to take more into account, though he critiques them too. His own solutions are religious or theological in the sense of showing that they require starting points that some would reject because of contrary "faith" commitments. Purpose and creation, in particular, may be a more acceptable notion (since Big Bang cosmology) than it was in Aristotle's time, or even in Niebuhr's. It may still be too big a stretch for those who expect philosophy to bring everything within the compass of rationalism. So he subjects rationalism to criticism.

4. George M. Marsden, *The Outrageous Idea of Christian Scholarship* (New York: Oxford University Press, 1997), 10–13.
5. Reinhold Niebuhr, *The Nature and Destiny of Man: Volume 1, Human Nature* (1941; reprint, New York: Charles Scribner's, 1964).

Charles Taylor's more recent *Sources of the Self: The Making of the Modern Identity* is another classic example of how a Christian scholar can recover resources that secularist scholars would neglect or avoid. Significantly, a critical point in his account of the long history of Western views of human identity is St. Augustine's "radical reflexivity."[6] Taylor is more explicitly philosophical (less theological) than Niebuhr, which shows that religious thinkers do not all parrot a common, alien dogmatism. They may disagree and yet still add to our thinking. Scholars might imagine they would have to "make allowances" for the "sectarian" views of even such eminent scholars. Yet the Gifford Lectures, which regularly call on religious scholars, are famous for discussing these subjects.[7]

Though it has been culturally impoverishing to reject views simply because of their theological or religious origins, I am not suggesting that they be given special treatment. It is jarring to find Niebuhr saying that Christianity represents the "highest development" of "both the idea and the fact of individuality."[8] But he only means that Christian intellectual traditions produced our views of individuality in the first place, as Taylor also attests. Naturally those traditions will be positioned to make the best sense of the concept.

Indeed, Niebuhr indicates why our ultimate statement on the human will be a theological one. Building on Heidegger's (Augustinian) realization that humans transcend even rationality, and on Kierkegaard's (Pauline) description of the paradox of human freedom, Niebuhr is succinct.

> Implicit in the human situation of freedom and in man's capacity to transcend himself and his world is his inability to construct a world of meaning without finding a source and key to the structure of meaning which transcends the world beyond his own capacity to transcend it. The problem of meaning, which is the basic problem of religion, transcends the ordinary rational problem of tracing the relation of things

6. Charles Taylor, *Sources of the Self: The Making of the Modern Identity* (Cambridge, MA: Harvard University Press, 1989), 131.
7. On the Gifford Lectures, see Stanley Hauerwas, *With the Grain of the Universe* (Grand Rapids, MI: Brazos, 2001).
8. Niebuhr, *The Nature and Destiny of Man*, 1:57.

to each other, as the freedom of man's spirit transcends his rational faculties.

This problem is not solved without the introduction of a principle of meaning which transcends the world of meaning to be interpreted. If some vitality of existence, or even some subordinate principle of coherence is used as the principle of meaning, man is involved in idolatry. He lifts some finite and contingent element of existence into the eminence of the divine. He uses something which itself requires explanation as the ultimate principle of coherence and meaning. . . . The fact of self-transcendence leads inevitably to the search for a God who transcends the world.[9]

Marsden thinks there are several other topics that Christian scholars would show a special affinity for. An understanding of activists who were motivated, or artists who were inspired, by their religion might benefit from a scholar's religious sympathies. Spotting the ideological nature of philosophies and of scholarship itself will come more naturally to those who have been marginalized for their religious beliefs. And generally, Marsden thinks that "cultural critique" is natural to religious perspectives in scholarship and instruction.[10] After all, a critical stance follows naturally from our standard nominal definition of "religion"; in English, "religion" means that which gives access to something beyond the ordinary. In former centuries Christianity often filled an intellectually constructive role, but more recently it has assumed a critical and prophetic stance witnessing to a transcending reality. Greater religious sensibility might also show how criticism could become constructive, in treating humility and charity as academic virtues. Finally, Marsden wonders how the academic concern over human rights can survive a deconstructing of the idea of humanity: "Christian theism . . . provides grounds for supporting the moral intuitions that many academics share."[11]

Nevertheless, religious scholars must be challenged to think much further about how to enter into dialogue. Even if we can identify the contributions religions can make, one must learn how to phrase them in ways that will show the connection. While some distinctively Chris-

---

9. Ibid., 162–165.
10. Marsden, *Outrageous Idea of Christian Scholarship*, 63–65, 72, 79.
11. Ibid., 87.

tian doctrines are relevant to current debates, one would need a new vocabulary to win a hearing for them today. "Sin," "trinity," "incarnation," and "creation" are words that would be greeted with incomprehension in the academy today. Yet they are all pregnant with meaning for our debates. To introduce them into discussion under antique terms will invite rejection.

As an example, one could show the significance of trinitarian notions to Azar Nafisi's fascinating memoir, *Reading Lolita in Tehran*. Islam has trouble tolerating her beloved novels (as opposed to fables), because the essential point of novels is to explore character development and personal relations.[12] American audiences, by contrast, cannot understand a religion that sees the individual only through the prism of law, to the point that an interest in personality seems a distraction from ultimate concerns. In Western culture it was the notion of the Trinity that gave personality its ultimacy, in the divine realm no less than the human. Christianity has a place for law but is not essentially a religion of law. The Western character of the novel is quite pronounced, as Walker Percy once pointed out.

> The Christian ethos sustains the narrative enterprise in ways so familiar to us that they can be overlooked. It underwrites those very properties of the novel without which there is no novel: I am speaking of the mystery of human life, its sense of predicament, of something having gone wrong, of life as a wayfaring and a pilgrimage, of the density and linearity of time and the sacramental reality of things.[13]

In his classic study of *The Rise of the Novel*, Ian Watt explains how the novel developed out of Puritan spiritual autobiography, of all things.[14] So, as it turns out, doctrines of the trinity, the incarnation, and spiritual conversion are still at the basis of some of the world's most intractable social and cultural differences. A vulgarization of these is-

---

12. Azar Nafisi, *Reading Lolita in Tehran* (New York: Random House, 2003), 194, 236, 268, 307.

13. Walker Percy, *Signposts in a Strange Land* (New York: Picador, 1991), 178.

14. Ian Watt, *The Rise of the Novel* (Berkeley: University of California Press, 1957), 15, 50, 75–84.

sues by unsympathetic professors would not help us make sense of our situation in the midst of religious globalization.

Theological doctrines of the image of God, incarnation, and creation deal with the mystery of human transcendence. Secularists might find what theologians like Emil Brunner have said on these matters quite evocative. Unfortunately, forcing theology off campus means we will have to play catch-up. One may imagine that the theologians long ago cast their definitions in concrete. But Christians, at least, do not think it discredits theology that it is still a work in progress, any more than it discredits science to think that it may be just beginning.

The idea of religion being allowed into academic debates will strike many as outlandish. Partly, that could reflect our simplistic notions of what religious arguments would be like. Those whose last brush with religion was in Sunday school may be underestimating them.

For example, one might assume that a Christian will argue mechanically from authoritative texts. Academics would naturally complain that there is no way to argue with those who cannot question their scriptures. Religions are generally thought to be tight propositional systems that seal minds off, what philosophers like John Rawls call "comprehensive views." This may be why many prefer to call themselves "spiritual but not religious."

Here is an example of the type of argument that would be objectionable. The Bible teaches that humanity is subject to sin; it follows that human governments will be untrustworthy and selfish, so we should be suspicious of our government's promotion of some war. This is awkward because it shows how one could come to the "right" conclusion but in the wrong way. It is a fallacious argument, critics would say, because it starts from the wrong place. Secularists would ask why they should treat the Bible as authoritative or accept the concept of sin as meaningful. They will insist that one justify these things on the basis of their secularist assumptions. For any intellectual argument must be on the basis of shared assumptions, to which both sides can appeal. Only then can we deploy our facts and our logic.

The beauty of secular arguments, they would say, is that we can all agree on them, given our common rationality. The problem with this view, however, is that religious people may not agree to the supposedly agreed viewpoint, say naturalism or scientism. Beyond that, we might have a hard time saying whether a given argument was religious or secular, especially where this involved the human.

By contrast to the kind of simplistic argument just offered, we note that religion may offer perspectives rather than propositions. Jesus, for example, was apparently drawn toward a Socratic mode. Beginning with questions, one continues until the other person attains a new insight. It is not an exercise of argumentative power over one's opponent, as in the standard model, but more a model of discovery. Jesus thought, apparently, that his hearers might discover something if they were honest with themselves.

We might try the same. X says, do you believe that the concept of "justice" is meaningful or not? Y may say no, it is only a justification of power. X then says, Can you live with the view that might is always right? Y might then begin thinking along unfamiliar lines. But if Y originally said yes, I believe in justice, then X asks whether that means that people should be treated as ends and not as means? If Y says yes again, X asks whether treating people as ends implies an absolute difference between humans and animals. Doesn't it imply that justice transcends naturalism, since there is no possibility of treating all (nonhuman) life-forms as ends? X hasn't told her opponent what to think or treated him as an opponent. She has just probed his assumptions. Like Jesus, she has tried to win the person, more than the argument.

One can't say how such arguments will play out. Both X and Y might change. The most striking thing about such arguments is that they may engage differing philosophies, faiths, and assumptions and yet be coherent. A rationalist can't refuse the discussion on the basis that he doesn't accept his opponent's premises, for they are not at issue. Yet X has brought him to the point of an existential and not simply an intellectual decision. Jesus sensed that his opponents wanted to argue over facts of the law when he wanted to get at something deeper. Such arguments should not be out of place in universities. They could awaken others to their basic views and show how to build on them rather than how to dismantle them.

One might ask whether my example above was really a religious argument. It did not argue from any particular religious beliefs. But Socratic arguments may uncover assumptions that are religious. They are good at opening one's mind to ultimate questions, which invite religious answers. Learning to deal with them, rather than dismissing them by the canons of secularism, is a challenge for the university.

Arguments in the humanities will be impossibly crippled if they cannot involve religious concepts, as in the example of historical scholarship. The basic assumptions of academic history come from Jewish and Christian sources. They don't come from Greek or Roman precedents, so we can't say they are self-evident. But I could list six of them. (1) Modern historians always look for the most discreditable motive possible. They are not satisfied until they can find a selfish motive (the technical meaning of "depravity"). Roman historians would have preferred discovering human nobility, without seeing it as a mark of special grace. (2) We view history as linear, not as cyclical or chaotic or repetitive. When we speak of development (as we constantly do), we are in what is called the Deuteronomic tradition, an Old Testament theme. (3) We are interested in the judgment of history within our narratives. We would lose all interest in history, as would our students, if we could not take sides. (4) On the other hand, we are skeptical of the idea of progress, of some positive evolutionary principle built into history. We understand that all those "developments" cost something and may even bankrupt us. And that all history is equidistant from eternity. (5) We believe humans are free beings, moral agents. As we have said, there was once talk of making history a social science, resting on determinist assumptions. That has been given up, as impossible and uninteresting. (6) And we are great ironists. Irony, the amusement at seeing humans fail at being Godlike, is a very Christian perspective.[15]

Epistemologically, these may not seem very impressive principles. Practically speaking, they trump epistemology. Here is one of those points at which Christianity became embedded in the academy. As we argued in chapter 2, this is true wherever in the university we deal with

15. Reinhold Niebuhr, "Humour and Faith," in *The Essential Reinhold Niebuhr*, ed. Robert McAfee Brown (New Haven: Yale University Press, 1986), 49–60.

human categories. We have long made the mistake of considering humanism to be a challenge to religion. Now religious persons may recognize humanists as allies in the face-off with naturalism.

Secular methods of inquiry do best with more limited questions. We started in this direction in the medieval university, which taught us not to multiply hypotheses beyond necessity (Occam's razor). But when we reach the frontiers, our debates begin to sound religious. At the risk of parodying our public arguments, imagine that I argue that murder should be decriminalized. After all, I say, our laws haven't stopped murders from occurring, which makes government look weak. Besides, some bioethicists think the concept of human is somewhat artificial, and without it murder loses its meaning. You say, but what if everybody were to start murdering people? And I say, that's not likely; it wasn't mainly the laws that kept people from murdering. Besides, who said that ethics has to be the same for everyone? You say, but that's the very basis of both religion and deontological ethics. I say, but we're just talking about law, not philosophy.

So you've run out of the standard arguments without convincing me, and in exasperation you say you wouldn't want to live in a society that didn't make an issue of murder, whatever I say. In short, you have reached the point at which you affirm something just because it is good or right. You may have discovered your kinship with those who don't want to live in a society that considers human fetuses as of no significance. Every step in that argument offered serious opportunities for religious elaborations.

Or take an even more extreme example. Say that under the impressions left by religious experience some of us object to eating human flesh. We go further, and object to *anyone* in our society eating human flesh, and pass laws against it. Thus we challenge someone's "right" to eat her dead child, if she bizarrely asserted that right. She might argue that our objection was religiously based, because there was no relevant secular argument that fit the case. Obviously, the supposed health issue is just a disguise for some old religious taboo, so long as it was properly cooked. Rationalists might find themselves in uneasy alliance with the religious, not knowing what would count as a secular-rational objection to this assertion of individual right.

Courts have been faced with the question of the disposal of aborted

fetuses. They have voided democratically passed laws requiring digni-
fied burial, for fear of establishing a religious observance. Philosophers
might hold that no allowable arguments could settle the matter, because
the terms would not have universally accepted meanings. But the secular view undemocratically enforced by the courts is not universally
accepted either.

Religious persons may object to secularist arguments because they
have outgrown them. After all, a secular awareness is more limited than
a religious one. Rudolf Otto and others remind us that we recognize the
transcendent only against the prior background of ordinary existence.
Religious experience is discovered as something incongruous within
ordinary reality and seeming to transcend it. So it takes more into account than a secular outlook would: things like personality, which science has trouble with.

Students who recognize that I am sympathetic to the sort of views
I'm voicing here sometimes seek me out with stories of slighting treatment they meet in the secular classroom as they struggle to understand
and present their religious views. It is not as though their professors'
worldviews are coherent either, but a certain dismissiveness is tolerated
in connection with religion. Sociologist Robert Wuthnow thinks some
of it could be viewed as "boundary maintenance behavior," when scholars feel a little insecure within their disciplines. They mark their territory by identifying outsiders and shunning them, in order to maintain
their own distinctiveness. Wuthnow thinks this especially infects his
fellow social scientists. If their identity as scientists is shaky, they may
react by being adamant in their rejection of others. He thinks this could
account for their registering markedly more secularist views than do
physicists and chemists, whose scientific credentials are more secure.[16]

If there is anything to that, it may explain why universities seem
more and more determined about their secularism. A sense of the marginalization of our universities may be making the professoriat impa-

16. Robert Wuthnow, "Science and the Sacred," in *The Sacred in a Secular Age: Toward
Revision in the Scientific Study of Religion*, ed. Phillip E. Hammond (Berkeley: University of California Press, 1985), 190, 196–199.

tient and off-hand. Academics may moralize about how it is wrong to define oneself against some "Other." But professors have their own Other, and for fifty years it has been the religious. In the process, they have frowned away religious viewpoints that would have opened a window toward the rest of society.

Churches have responded in kind, picturing universities as deserts of infidelity. Healing might begin in the Christian study centers formed at several universities, where faculty and students sharpen their sense of what religious perspectives have to offer to the stalled debates on their campuses. They might foster the virtues of humility and respect that could be recommended to the university generally.[17] And while Christian theology parted company with scholarship a century ago when theology was in a soft period, secular scholars might relate more naturally to the neo-orthodoxy of the 1940s or the radical orthodoxy or narrative theology current today.

As must be clear by now, I do not presume to say what a more inclusive university should teach. That would be to decide in advance what the outcome of discovery will be. This is what I would criticize in the secularist university, a determination to anticipate what form its discoveries must take.

Respecting the religious viewpoints of students or professors, rather than simply fending them off, could enrich academic debates. After all, the central question in medicine is a spiritual one. The concepts of disease and insanity embody values that originated in religious worldviews, not in naturalism. Persons in those fields are responding to a religious call whether they are aware of it or not.

The central problem in law is a doctrinal one, a question of how we should relate to each other. The recent concentration on "rights" is an awkward way of approximating an ethical order when we don't recognize religious values or virtues. As an effort to correct the deficiencies of an earlier order, it is proving to have problems of its own.

Some of the world's great music, art, architecture, poetry, drama and fiction is even now being produced under the inspiration of religion.

17. The Web site of the center near my university is at www.christianstudycenter.org.

Serious composers of real (not commercial) music are producing large amounts of music that tries to express religious themes. Church building inspires architects who are tired of creating temples to money. Writers in many languages are producing literature that explores religious themes at a Nobel Prize level.

Education is a fundamentally religious enterprise. It must be built on foundations of belief, since there are no self-validating rational principles. And all forms of instruction turn out to have some basis in indoctrination. The central concept of business is a spiritual one. The term "wealth" does not primarily mean money. It means "weal" or "well-being," which ultimately involves religious perspectives. Money is only a means toward this end, and if we have no idea what well-being is, money will not help us get there.

The central problem of government administration is a theological one, being the question of individual and social well-being. Governments regularly go well beyond anything a secular or utilitarian philosophy could justify, and they could acknowledge this fact by allowing religious arguments into political discussion.

Even the central question about science is a religious one. It is the question of what use to make of our knowledge. This isn't part of the scientist's kit, but there would be no reason for science if such knowledge was pointless.

Students who thought that religion addressed only spiritual questions need to know that all their majors involve spiritual questions. They shouldn't leave college without considering them.

11

POSTSECULARISM AND THE UNIVERSITY

A century ago American society and education seemed to have a common project, unified by a concept of modernity. The culture found some agreement on which were the important books, musical compositions, and artists and on how they differed from the merely commercial ones. Or at least we expected these points to be seriously argued. As late as the 1960s historian Richard Hofstadter could assume a forward intellectual movement represented by artistic modernism, Freudianism, Marxism, Keynesianism, moral relativism, and secular rationalism.[1] Each branch of culture was thought to be following a main stem of development, reaching toward greater truth or honesty or simplicity. It might not be immediately clear which was the main stem and which were the offshoots that would wither and fall away. So critics argued such matters from some principle that seemed convincing, like reality or sincerity. At least in looking back they thought they could discern an arrow of development and a canon of classics in art and thought. For decades our intellectual leaders were able to maintain a devotion to experimental music and art and poetry that were utterly puzzling to the public, convincing us that the future would validate their insights. The public could hope to follow these debates through nothing more esoteric than *Life* magazine and the national radio networks. Within the

1. Richard Hofstadter, *Anti-Intellectualism in American Life* (New York: Alfred A. Knopf, 1963), 43, 47.

academy, too, the main questions were agreed on and the important participants had been identified.

Nowadays, little of this confidence is left, and there seem to be walls sealing the university off from the public. Through the 1990s the journal *Lingua Franca* tried to create a wider conversation among academics. Their most interesting articles described the antics and the shrill tone of those who thought the stakes were still high. But the public had lost what interest it ever had, and even the academic audience for this lively publication could not sustain it.[2]

Journalists continue to encourage the notion that the United States is a single society and culture. Of course, they have a financial stake in whether we stay in step by following the stories they're reporting. It is natural for them to present our conflicts as something to be overcome and to assume that there are recognized principles, like secular liberalism, to help in settling the issues. But the increasing appeal to tolerance itself may show that the hope of real agreement is waning. In the meantime, as debate fails us, we increasingly appeal to fashion. An academic elite finds it ever harder to maintain any kind of leadership.

Thus we may be seeing the disintegration of a single American culture. The culture wars since the 1980s have resulted in something like a standoff. The media have become increasingly "liberal" by their own self-report,[3] but they have also broken ranks. Television news outlets have begun attacking each other, to the amusement and enlightenment of their dwindling audience. A more serious decline is seen in the increasingly trivial character of news product since the Cold War, as news outlets become more easily distracted by the entertainment value of crime and sex. Religions also, which used to be part of the public sphere, are more satisfied to be fenced into the private sphere, though we note that this is where our media are focusing more of their attention.

While the networks have announced that we are all minorities now, this has not really sunk in. The ideal of the common school still enjoys popular support, so that the media can present attacks on the govern-

---

2. Alexander Star, ed., *Quick Studies: The Best of Lingua Franca* (New York: Farrar, Straus and Giroux, 2002), xxvi.

3. *U.S. News and World Report*, 7 June 2004, 12, reports a Pew Survey which shows self-identified liberals up from 22 to 34 percent since 1995, pulling the "moderate" category in that direction. Only 7 percent of reporters and editors thought of themselves as conservative.

ment's educational monopoly as threatening. Yet schools show little confidence that they know what is vital for students to learn. In the nineteenth century government schools were valued for promoting a common culture. Now they think it their duty to challenge the common culture, tattered as it is, in the name of multiculturalism and diversity. This has led to a constituency in favor of private schools and tax vouchers. So far, however, concerns over social cohesion are blocking such initiatives.

Educational elites have reason to worry about this more divisive situation. Students and parents put up some resistance to a countercultural curriculum. The secularist hope that a rationalism purged of traditional elements could be the universal language of all knowledge and professional expertise has played out and has left us in a place we hardly recognize. I have called our situation "postsecularist" and defined it as a condition in which fashion has replaced debate, ending in that "marketplace of ideas" we hear about.

The thing about fashion is that there doesn't seem any rhyme or reason to it.[4] Fashion is the indeterminacy principle at the level of our lifeworld. Whatever the dynamics of a marketplace, they are different from the dialectic that was expected to ensure rational progress. I have tried to argue that reviving debate would require that we include some of the elements we have tried to do without. a more searching consideration of the human, of standards of value and judgment. Beyond this, we need to foster an intellectual culture that puts respect, appreciation, and humility on the same level as the one remaining academic virtue of suspicion.

The force behind postsecularism is largely the media, and specifically its daily character.[5] Dailiness makes it difficult to focus on the big questions, given the distractions that keep popping up. As journalism

4. Malcolm Gladwell, *The Tipping Point: How Little Things Can Make a Big Difference* (Boston: Little, Brown, 2000), shows that we can only discuss the dynamics but not the causes of changes in fashion.

5. The following is elaborated in my *The News Revolution in England: Cultural Dynamics of Daily Information* (New York: Oxford University Press, 1996) and *How the News Makes Us Dumb: The Death of Wisdom in an Information Society* (Downers Grove, IL: InterVarsity, 1999).

drops all pretensions to being a profession and becomes more frankly a business, it is more obviously guided by profits rather than significance. Universities could be acting as an anchor, dragging against the journalistic currents. But the news vending machines on campus seem as prominent as the bookstore, filled with mugs and sweatshirts.

In the 1960s, intellectuals and even the public talked a lot about Marshall McLuhan's theory of a print revolution at the beginning of modern history, which he explained in books like *The Gutenberg Galaxy* and *Understanding Media*. The theory was that in the sixteenth century printing had decisively changed the way Western minds worked. Print promoted rationality, factual discourse, and linear thinking by fixing subjects so that they didn't get too slippery for careful dissection. Print had revolutionized Western society, secularizing culture and encouraging science.

McLuhan went on to point out that we were even then watching another revolution overtake the print revolution. An electronic revolution was encouraging TV and films to undermine print culture, leading to a kind of secondary orality. What McLuhan didn't notice was that the essential feature of this electronic revolution had long been present in daily publication. Periodical publication had imperceptibly created a *news consciousness*, a fixation on daily trends and fashions instead of more comprehensive treatments of significant subjects. Over three centuries news schedules had driven philosophy and such to the margins of culture.

Newspapers and books are both printed, to be sure, but they are not the same in their effect. Newspapers are the opposite of books, taking things apart rather than putting them together. You must disassemble reality if you want to make a business of selling information. There must be a new issue or broadcast every day, whether or not the world has turned a corner. Even if journalists are following an old story, they must go a new direction with it each day. If they can't, they must switch our attention to something else.

One might think this is just being realistic, recognizing that there is a new world out there every day. But there is also an old world out there every day, which is by definition not news. It would be a mistake to suppose that a daily ration of excitement is the natural course of things. The exciting world of the news is a manufactured product. If we were used to calling it "news product," we wouldn't mistake it for part of nature. But at the moment, universities don't seem eager to fight the idea that news is a shortcut to wisdom.

The word "wisdom" is seldom used around universities. University presidents talk in terms of information. Legislators who feel that more leadership is needed set goals and assessment guidelines for universities that do not presume to involve wisdom or judgment. Students may come to university to explore ideas, but they settle for learning which attitudes are current in a secular culture.

Universities began in a world that now seems remote in its simplicity. They looked forward to completing the sciences and turning as much of their curriculum as possible into science. Nobody in 1900 would have thought that anything as ephemeral as news would have a place in the ivory tower. But as universities complicated all questions, information exploded out of their laboratories and seminars and research carrels. No one was in charge of integrating all this into a coherent view of life.

Just as our public schools' main job is to counteract the effects of our entertainment industry, so universities could see their job as battling the news industry. Instead they take news consciousness as a fact of life. Odd as it may seem, they frequently invite news-readers to campus to get their wisdom on our situation. Perhaps this is because theirs are the only big names our students know. Universities tell students they need to pay attention to the news to be "informed." Harvard used to invite its applicants to discuss what news sources they used, as a subject for their application essays. Davidson College used to tell the students it accepted to read the *Washington Post* all summer before they arrived, when they had all the world's literature to choose from.

My university issues faculty members "A Guide to Working with the Media." It warns that "reporters are usually under extremely tight deadlines, and a delay of a day, or even an hour, can mean the difference between favorable coverage and a lost opportunity or a reporter disinclined to turn to our university for help." I doubt that our philosophy department has ever been of help here. Even if they were asked, they would be defeated by the fact that—as the guide warns—"Few sound bites are more than 20 seconds long."

⌒

Sadly, university and news elites seem to think they have a responsibility to combat lagging cultural expressions. Of course, culture is what society depends on to orient us, creating our second nature. Even universities are quite respectful of alien cultures. They treat our own as an enemy because, to be sure, culture can be confining and can limit our horizons and our freedoms. The news industry, likewise, is always on the lookout for something else to put in play. We have learned a bunch of bad names for culture—master-texts, meta-narratives, ideologies, religions, foundationalisms, myths. Cultural studies departments have the job of unmasking whatever seems settled.

After taking culture apart, who is there to put it back together? Who is in charge of appreciation or respect these days? If these are as important as analysis and criticism, then one can see why the public sees the tone on campuses as negative and irrelevant. Academics might counter that ultimately we can't ignore the nihilism that opens at the end of philosophy.

Actually, they are ignoring challenges to that view, like philosopher John Milbank's *Theology and Social Theory: Beyond Secular Reason*. His book is a Christian answer in the sense that Milbank is a Christian and brings unaccustomed perspectives to bear. Milbank may be a difficult read, but he can be ignored only on the basis that one dare not admit religious arguments into the antiseptic environment that secularism has created. My point is that it has taken someone who did not share the reigning academic culture to develop arguments indicating that nihilism may not yawn at the end of all thought. It will take outsiders to see the artificiality of academic rationalism.

Professor Martha Nussbaum shows how even the most generous-minded academics can be blind toward possible contributions from religion. In the midst of a work pleading for diversity of all kinds, when it comes to religion she baulks. Though she thinks it is vital to have some knowledge of unfamiliar religions, she sees only problems when students are loyal toward their own. While she affirms all other groups, the one that ought to become more like the rest of us are the fundamentalists. Considering religious colleges, she wonders how they can guarantee free inquiry and curricular diversity. She doesn't worry about secular colleges in that regard, hinting that secular institutions don't hesitate to discriminate against certain religious groups in their hiring.[6] So we are not alerted to how many perspectives are kept off campus by a legally encouraged precensorship. All this goes back to the fact that academics do not think that religious arguments would ever actually contribute, let alone prevail, in intellectual debate. This despite the fact that many of their own assumptions turn out to be fundamentally religious.

If all that one saw of religion was what appears on American television, my appeal for religious voices in the academy would surely be puzzling. But the circus atmosphere that surrounds so much of it provides evidence that religion can operate in a decadent marketplace. It cannot be at its healthiest when that is the case. We might even hope that universities will make religion a more serious and intelligent area of our lives. They could find themselves more at the heart of our national life if they fostered an atmosphere of real exploration of concerns that the population has never given up.

Comparative literature professor David Damrosch, in a recent discussion of the need for a more collaborative university culture, can see that religion is part of his theme. One of his targets is Allan Bloom, whose *The Closing of the American Mind* (1987) exhibited what Damrosch calls a "militant secularism." He thinks Bloom misunderstood even his beloved Greeks because he was blinded toward their religion. For instance, if he had treated the Bible as more than "a prelude to Dante" in his Great Books curriculum, Bloom might have been able to see vital parallels in Plato as well. Even with his Jewish sensibilities on the subject, Damrosch wonders whether "the university can perhaps better be seen in symbiosis with religion rather than in opposition to it."[7] He does not, of course, just mean to increase the popularity of universities in a culture that apparently discounts them, but also to make them truer to their purpose in fostering wisdom.

6. Martha C. Nussbaum, *Cultivating Humanity: A Classical Defense of Reform in Liberal Education* (Cambridge, MA: Harvard University Press, 1997), 261–269.
7. David Damrosch, *We Scholars: Changing the Culture of the University* (Cambridge, MA: Harvard University Press, 1995), 111–119.

12

A Vision of the Future

I invite you to imagine universities that are incidentally secular in the sense that religion doesn't rule, but not officially secularist in the sense that religion is ruled out: universities whose goal is not to impose a privileged viewpoint but to understand all viewpoints that are able to win a hearing.

Imagine universities that openly acknowledge that humans are the most interesting things in creation, and that make it their goal to explore the implications of this view. Think of placing that goal on the same level as measuring the age of rocks, or dissolving cultures into power relations, or assuring us that our consciousness will eventually be explained in physicalist terms.

Imagine taking "Know thyself" as a central educational goal, rather than working to alienate students from their cultural backgrounds. Further, think of recognizing the human and the personal as religious, whatever else they are, and being willing to consider theological scholarship in exploring that understanding.

Imagine the university being frank and relaxed about arguments over moral judgments, rather than just insinuating them. And think of professional schools taking on real educational significance as they learn to relate to serious debates on human needs.

Imagine accreditation agencies that do not think their job is to enforce a secularist uniformity that they define as neutrality.

All this would require a different academic culture than that of our present universities. It would involve more a desire to listen than a compulsion toward single vision. But how likely is it? Will the reaction to such proposals be invidious comparisons with what secularists imagine of medieval universities, when theology was said to be the queen of the sciences? Will they be understood as suggesting that we turn the clock back instead of moving on from the hole we've fallen into?

What could induce present fashions to alter in this direction, rather than spiraling in further circles of rejection? Perhaps we could begin with a plea that students be treated with more respect than they may now receive. Proscribed views are what used to be called "heresy," and secular institutions, above all, should be embarrassed to be involved with such notions.

Of course, the other side of the coin is that religious students need to be smarter about the ways they present their beliefs if they want to make them relevant. It is hardly their fault that they don't see how a religious discourse could meet some of the university's concerns. They have not been taught that religion still underlies many academic disciplines. A serious reeducation would be necessary to that end. Some of that is even now going on in religious colleges and universities, which must take themselves more seriously.

Wherever there have been established churches there has been anticlericalism, because power will be resented. If universities now occupy the place of an established church in America, it will occasionally betray its disdain for public standards of thought. And it should therefore expect the opposition it now faces, most notably in stingy funding. For it is one thing to disregard students who ask the wrong thing; it is another to disregard legislators, taxpayers, donors, or voters. So generally we should imagine inviting silenced voices back into the discussion, to reverse the kinds of social and intellectual decline we've been talking about.

INDEX